FOREWORD

The two reports comprising this volume were prepared under the 1990 "Economic Barriers to Sound Environmental and Resource Management" activity of the OECD Environment Committee. The Environment Committee recommended (15th July, 1991) that these reports be made available to the public.

Both reports grew out of a series of case studies on market and intervention policy failures in several OECD countries. These case studies are available under the following titles:

Turner, R. and Jones, T. (eds.) (1991). *Wetlands: Market and Intervention Failures (Four Case Studies)*. Earthscan Publications: London, UK.

Jones, T. and Wibe, S. (eds.) (forthcoming, April 1992). *Forests: Market and Intervention Failures (Five Case Studies)*. Earthscan Publications: London, UK.

The intellectual contribution made by the authors of these case studies to this volume is gratefully acknowledged, as are the contributions of William Hyde (US Department of Agriculture, Washington), Jean de Montgolfier (CEMAGREF, Aix-en-Provence), Patrick Dugan (International Union for the Conservation of Nature, Geneva), Edward Maltby (University of Exeter, UK) and Claude Henri (Ecole Polytechnique, Paris).

The book is published on the responsibility of the Secretary General.

Market
and
Government
Failures
in
Environmental
Management

Wetlands and Forests

ORGANISATION FOR ECONOMIC CO-OPERATION AND DEVELOPMENT

ORGANISATION FOR ECONOMIC CO-OPERATION AND DEVELOPMENT

Pursuant to Article 1 of the Convention signed in Paris on 14th December 1960, and which came into force on 30th September 1961, the Organisation for Economic Co-operation and Development (OECD) shall promote policies designed:

— to achieve the highest sustainable economic growth and employment and a rising standard of living in Member countries, while maintaining financial stability, and thus to contribute to the development of the world economy;

— to contribute to sound economic expansion in Member as well as non-member countries in the process of economic development; and

— to contribute to the expansion of world trade on a multilateral, non-discriminatory basis in accordance with international obligations.

The original Member countries of the OECD are Austria, Belgium, Canada, Denmark, France, Germany, Greece, Iceland, Ireland, Italy, Luxembourg, the Netherlands, Norway, Portugal, Spain, Sweden, Switzerland, Turkey, the United Kingdom and the United States. The following countries became Members subsequently through accession at the dates indicated hereafter: Japan (28th April 1964), Finland (28th January 1969), Australia (7th June 1971) and New Zealand (29th May 1973). The Commission of the European Communities takes part in the work of the OECD (Article 13 of the OECD Convention). Yugoslavia has a special status at OECD (agreement of 28th October 1961).

Publié en français sous le titre :

LES DÉFAILLANCES DU MARCHÉ ET DES GOUVERNEMENTS
DANS LA GESTION DE L'ENVIRONNEMENT :
LES ZONES HUMIDES ET LES FORÊTS

Photo A. Galievsky/OECD

TABLE OF CONTENTS

PREFACE

In 1987, the World Commission on Environment and Development (better known as the Brundtland Commission) focussed global attention on the need for "sustainable economic development". The central message from the Brundtland Commission was that this objective could best be achieved through a full partnership between environmental and economic interests.

Recent world events have clearly demonstrated that market-based economic systems are the most appropriate framework in which to develop that partnership. Clearly, markets have their shortcomings in resolving both environmental and economic problems, but no other system has yet been suggested that delivers better prospects for economic prosperity, coupled with a healthy environment.

As one example, in the 1960s, the need for quick action on the environment prompted many governments to adopt regulatory approaches to solving their environmental problems. It is becoming increasingly clear, however, that "command and control" approaches are not always the best option. They tend to be excessively costly in economic terms, and they do not inherently promote the long term solutions that some environmental problems require. Consequently, along with an unprecedented level of public concern about environmental problems, has come an unprecedented level of interest in the potential of markets to provide the answers.

But can markets deliver what is being asked of them? Arguably, the single most important factor in the applying market principles to the environmental resource allocation problem is "getting the prices right". Unless prices for raw materials and products properly reflect their full social costs, and unless prices are assigned to those environmental resources (air, water, wildlife, and land) that presently serve as cost-free receptacles for society's wastes, these resources will be inefficiently used, envronmental pollution will increase, and real economic growth will inevitably be lower than it could otherwise have been.

Full social costing will ultimately depend on the values that society places on its environmental resources. One can argue about *how* to value the environment, but of the *need* to value it in making allocation decisions, there can be no doubt. The only real issue is how that valuation will occur. (Note that not allowing any use of environmental resources at all is the same thing as valuing that resource infinitely, and allowing unlimited use is the same thing as valuing that resource at zero).

Some social values may be readily expressed in the market-place. Most will not. Where they are not, we can say that a "market failure" has occurred. In a very real sense, we can say that the market has "failed" to send the right signals to decision-makers. Another reason why markets fail to produce "correct" price signals is the so-called "public goods problem". In this situation, the fact that environmental resources cannot be "owned" by anyone means that

7

no one will feel obliged to act in the best interests of the environment. Other forms of market failure exist, but these are the two most common generic forms of the problem.

An extended cost-benefit approach seems to offer one way of overcoming this problem. By forcing the environmental and economic tradeoffs to be considered as part of the same assessment, at least the implicit values being used by the decision-makers can be made more explicit. Put another way, cost-benefit analysis can be a valuable way of getting the environmental message across to economic managers, and of getting the economic message across to environmental managers. Cost-benefit analysis does not solve all the analytical problems (distributional issues being an obvious example), but properly used, it can provide some interesting insights for decision-makers.

To "correct" market failures, governments often step in with policies or programmes of their own. Unfortunately, these government activities may or may not achieve their intended objectives. In addition, policies designed for one sector of government interest may have unintended and negative impacts on other sectors. Both of these situations are examples of what might be called "policy intervention failures", and both are rooted in the fact that appropriate price signals are not readily available to guide governments in designing their policies.

In 1988, the Organisation for Economic Cooperation and Development (OECD) launched a study on "Overcoming Impediments to the Integration of Environmental Considerations into Economic Development". This project was designed to look at market and government intervention failures in three important environmental sectors: transportation, wetlands, and forests. The underlying premise of these studies was that the elimination of market and intervention failures would ultimately mean *both* better environmental management *and* better prospects for economic growth. This "win-win" situation is precisely the kind of partnership that the Brundtland Commission called for in its final report.

Each of the three OECD study areas (transportation, wetlands, forestry) began with a series of individual country case studies. These case studies describe the various market and intervention failures that exist in each country, and they suggest possible ways of correcting these failures. Upon completion of the case studies, summary reports were prepared for each of the three broad study areas. This volume presents the results of the wetlands and forestry summary reports.

Chapter 1

POLICY FAILURES IN MANAGING WETLANDS

by R. Kerry Turner*

* Dr. Turner is the Executive Director of the Centre for Social and Economic Research on the Global Environment (CSERGE), University of East Anglia, Norwich, and University College, London, UK. He has served as an economic consultant to several UK agencies and international bodies, and he has published widely on various topics in the field of environmental economics.

BACKGROUND

The two main objectives of this report are to lay out an appropriate methodological framework for the analysis of wetland management problems; and to bring together the key issues that emerged from four national case studies (for the United Kingdom, the United States, France and Spain) on the nature and extent of market and intervention failures in wetlands policy.

The notion of "sustainability" seems at first glance to be a relatively simple and sensible idea, that should receive almost universal support. But, as is often the case, first thoughts can be deceptive once the operational implications are considered. The large recent literature on sustainable growth and development contains an array of definitions and supporting arguments, some of which are contradictory (see Pearce, Markandya & Barbier, 1989; Pezzey, 1989; and Turner, 1988*a*).

Nevertheless, within the central core of the sustainable economic development concept is the idea that economic systems are dependent on ecological foundations and, ultimately, on the maintenance of the global waste assimilation and life-support systems. A vital principle of sustainable economics is that natural resources and environments are multifunctional, and represent vast storehouses of economic value.

Most definitions of sustainable development accept the "equity principle", that a non-declining (and unimpaired) stock of capital assets (in value terms) should be transferred from one generation to the next. According to this analysis, the aggregate stock is made up of three components: "Critical" Natural Capital $(K_N{}^C)$, "Other" Natural Capital (K_N) and "Man-Made" Capital (K_M). The $K_N{}^C$ category is composed of ecosystems and processes which are, by definition, of very high value.

If future generations are not to be made worse off by present-day activities, they require the same potential economic opportunities to achieve their welfare that the current generation enjoys. The portfolio of capital assets must therefore be managed in such a way as to maintain these potential opportunities. In other words, $K_N{}^C$ must be conserved and/or managed on a sustainable usage basis.

If kept in a conserved, natural/semi-natural state, wetlands are excellent examples of multi-functional resources. In other words, they are capital assets requiring appropriate valuation and management if they are to continue to produce a sustainable flow of outputs (commodity and service values).

It is argued in this report that, given past and on-going losses of wetlands, more attention needs to be paid to maintaining the balance between wetland conservation, sustainable utilisation, and wetland conversion. The main "sustainability principles" are outlined in the left-hand column of Figure 1.1, while the "practical management issues" for wetlands are set out in the

Figure 1.1. **Principles and Practice of Sustainable Development in the Wetlands Context**

Global On-Going Loss of Temperate and Tropical Wetlands

Sustainability Principles

Practice

Efficiency and equity within and between generations; efficiency and equity objectives are secured by actual compensation; rejection of potential welfare concept

Balance to be struck between wetland conservation, sustainable utilisation and economic development; sustainable utilisation the key concept for wetlands in those countries in which wetlands have already been heavily transformed by human intervention. Conservation is the priority for countries which still retain extensive areas of relatively unmodified wetlands; and conservation of high value wetlands is a priority in all countries. NO NET-LOSS PRINCIPLE the basic policy objective.

Much Environmental Degradation is due to a combination of Information, Market and Intervention Failures

Wetlands loss rate is high and has been caused by 'natural' resource use conflict together with information, market and intervention failures, *i.e.* lack of awareness and appreciation of the full value of wetlands; pollution damage and overutilisation because of open access; and inefficient or inconsistent policy.

Actual compensation is operationalised via three types of capital transfer in order to pass on a portfolio of productive opportunities of equal or greater value to the next generation:

"CRITICAL"   +   "OTHER"   +   "MAN-
NATURAL   NATURAL   MADE"
CAPITAL   CAPITAL   CAPITAL

K_N^C < VERY LIMITED > K_N < GREATER > K_M
        SUBSTITUTION   SUBSTITUTION

$K_N^C + K_N + K_M$ = TOTAL CAPITAL STOCK

Wetlands to be differentiated in terms of their structural and functional value; not all wetlands are equally valuable, but most are multifunctional assets with extensive environmental capacities/infrastructures; Wetlands Inventory (regional, national and international) required; identification of actual and potential threats to wetlands, because they are open systems, off-site water basin-wide analysis is required. No net-loss objective a relative not an absolute constraint, substitution possibilities.

Valuation of the Capital Stock: Total Economic Value = Use + Option + Existence Values

Total economic value of wetlands stock is very high; monetary valuation methods and techniques available for some but not yet all of the wetland functions and services.

Management of the multifunctional natural capital stock to ensure sustainable flow of income and conservation of the toal resource stock

Extended Cost-Benefit Analysis can provide a sound methodological base for sustainable resource management

On-going and Anticipatory Assessment Process; standard project appraisal methods augmented by shadow project analysis - wetland creation, transfer and restoration possibilities and costs; Integrated Water Basin Management is the longer-term objective, which will require CBA, plus other non-monetary assessment methods.

right-hand column of the same Figure. Each of these practical management issues are examined in more detail later in the report.

Five central questions will be addressed here:

1. What are wetlands, and what is their current status?
2. If (as seems likely) wetland loss rates continue to be significant, why should society be concerned? Are wetlands valuable, and can their worth be quantified in monetary terms?
3. Is it the case that valuable wetland resources are not being managed optimally (in economic terms), resulting in socially inefficient resource use?
4. If it is the case that such social inefficiency exists, what is the source(s) of the problem?
5. What can/should be done about the problem?

DEFINITIONS AND CURRENT STATUS

The term "wetland" can be applied to any part of the continuum between aquatic and terrestrial environments. The Convention on Wetlands of International Importance (Ramsar Convention) offers the following definition: "areas of marshes, fen, peatland or water, whether natural or artificial, permanent or temporary, with water that is static or flowing, fresh, brackish or salt, including areas of marine water the depth of which at low-tide does not exceed six metres".

The most comprehensive classification system (Cowardin System) is based on such factors as: the salinity and pH of wetlands; the characteristic vegetation and dominant plant species; the frequency and duration of flooding; and the organic or mineral composition of soils. On this basis, wetlands are defined as lands transitional between terrestrial and aquatic systems, where the water table is usually at or near the surface, or the land is covered by shallow water. The dominant factor is an excess of water. The degree of water permanence determines the nature of soil development and the types of plant and animal communities living at the soil surface. Five wetland ecosystems are usually recognised: marine, estuarine, riverine, lacustrine and marsh/bog/swamp.

Using the factors "location" (coastal or inland), "salinity" (freshwater or saltwater), and "dominant vegetation" (marsh, swamp or bog), ten basic categories of wetland can be distinguished – see Table 1.1.

Wetland ecosystems account for about 6 per cent of global land area, and are considered by many authorities to be among the most threatened of all environmental resources. During the 20th century, wetland loss rates generally have been very high. Both the physical extent of wetlands, and their quality (in terms of species diversity *etc.*) have been diminished over this period. Most of the physical losses have been due to the conversion of wetlands to other land uses (industrial, agricultural and residential). But qualitative degradation (chemical and biological) has also occurred in more subtle, complex, and longer term ways, due to air and water pollution, as well as to water supply diminution. The degradation risks faced by wetlands have been enhanced by the "open system" nature of these resources. This has made wetlands especially prone to damages caused by activities often located a considerable distance away from the wetland site, but still within the relevant drainage basin area.

Table 1.1. Wetland Types and Functions

Wetland Types	Wetland Functions/Services[1]
(Based on location, salinity and dominant vegetation)	(Based on wetland ecosystems' *physical,* and *chemical* and *biological* role in the biosphere).
a) Inland Freshwater Marshes	1) *(a,b,e,f,g)* Nutrient cycling and storage: resulting in potential water quality improvement.
b) Inland Saline Marshes	2) *(a,c,e,f,g)* Potential aquifer or groundwater storage and recharge function.
c) Bogs	3) (all, except perhaps *d)* Provision of a delay mechanism for the release of flood waters; storm protection from tidal surges and winds.
d) Tundra	4) *(a,b,g,h,i,j)* Shoreline anchoring (coastal and riverine) providing a buffer against erosion.
e) Shrub Swamp	5) (all) Ameliorating influences on local microclimates, and a possible biospherical stabilisation role, carbon sinks *etc.*
f) Wooded Swamps	6) (all, to varying degrees) Food web support (local and extended).
g) Wet Meadows, Bottomlands, and Other Riparian Habitats	7) (all, to varying degrees) Commercial outputs: fish, furs, timber, wildfowl, peat fuel, reed, low-intensity grazing.
h) Coastal Salt Marshes	8) (all, to varying degrees) Recreational opportunities.
i) Mangrove Swamps	9) (all, to varying degrees) Other, *e.g.* wildlife habitats, landscape assets. Non-use values are likely to be very significant for unique, high-rank order, wetlands.
j) Tidal Freshwater Marshes	

1. Functions/services 1 to 6 are natural wetland processes which yield indirect use values, despite the fact that these values are not reflected in market prices. The structure of wetland ecosystems also enables humans to gain direct use values in the form of commodities and other services (7, 8 & 9), some of which will be priced on markets. Finally, wetlands can produce non-use values. Humans may value the continuing existence of such natural/semi natural systems, even though no current or future use is actually anticipated.

While areas such as North America and Australia still retain significant and relatively pristine wetland stocks, these stocks are significantly reduced from what they once were. In most of Europe, the remaining wetland acreage is only a fraction of the original stock, and is close to (if not below) critical levels. Precise loss estimates on a national basis are, however, not available.

A number of OECD Member countries did implement some policy changes in the mid to late 1970s, which were designed to slow down or halt wetland conversion. The success (or otherwise) of these policy changes has not been monitored sufficiently for precise quantification to be possible. Nevertheless, there is a strong probability that wetland loss rates remain high in many OECD economies.

On the global scale, the extensive tropical wetland resources in developing economics are also undergoing increasing change as a result of improved access to wetland zones; of the pressures of population growth; and of general economic development. Extensive areas of tropical wetland have been (and continue to be) lost, either as a direct result of conversion to intensive agriculture, aquaculture or industrial use, or through more gradual qualitative changes caused by hydrological perturbation, pollution and unsustainable levels of grazing and fishing activities. Goodland and Ledec (1989) have remarked that, until two or three decades ago, a large proportion of the world's wildlands (including wetlands) were protected by their remoteness, their vastness and their marginal usefulness for agriculture or other economic activities. The last thirty years or so, however, have witnessed the rapid conversion of wetlands in all developing countries.

Mangrove swamps, for example, are rapidly disappearing throughout Asia and Africa, because of land reclamation, fishpond construction, mining and waste disposal. In the Philippines alone, some 300 000 ha (67 per cent of the national mangrove stock) were lost over the period 1920-1980. Other wetland types have suffered equally rapid losses. In Nigeria, for example, the floodplains of the Hadejia river have been reduced by over 300 km² as a result of dam construction. Quality degradation is also a growing problem, the majority of coastal wetlands in Brazil have been degraded as a result of pollution.

All the case studies (United Kingdom, United States, France and Spain) contain evidence to support the general presumption of continued wetland losses. In the United Kingdom, it has been claimed that some 150 000 acres of wetland were lost every year (during the 1970's and early 1980's), due solely to agricultural drainage and agricultural land use intensification. Between the early 1950s and the 1980s, some 15 per cent of the salt marshes (including 4 000 ha of sites of special scientific interest) in England and Wales were lost to agricultural and/or industrial land reclamation schemes. Some 84 per cent of Britain's raised bog had disappeared by 1978 because of afforestation, agricultural reclamation and commercial peat cutting.

In France, a number of important wetlands were drained during the period 1960-1985, including the Marais des Echets part of Les Dombes (near Lyon), Marais de St-Gond, Marais Communal de Vouillé, the Fecht Valley, and the marshes of the Landes de Gasgogne. Over roughly the same period, forty percent of the coastal wetlands of Brittany were also lost. This wetlands destruction process has continued throughout the 1980's and into 1990 in France, mainly due to on-going agricultural drainage and reclamation activities.

In the United States, some sources put national wetland loss rates at 400 000 to 500 000 acres per annum between 1950 and 1975, declining to 250 000 acres per annum after that. These national estimates are continuously being reviewed and revised, but evidence from regional and local studies indicates that significant wetland losses are still occurring. Most of the inland freshwater wetland losses (the dominant loss category) have been caused by conversion to agricultural activities. In the case of coastal wetlands, just over half the losses have been the result of dredging, port, marina and canal construction, together with physical erosion processes.

In Spain, about 60 per cent of the nation's original wetland surface area has been lost. In contrast to the experiences of the other case study countries, almost all of the Spanish wetland losses have occurred in the last 25 years.

Overall, despite the lack of precise national and global wetland loss data, it is reasonable to assume that such losses have been, and continue to be, significant. The next important question to pose then is, should society be concerned about the loss of such ecosystems? In order to answer this question, it is necessary to investigate the "value" of the total stock (or infrastructure) of wetlands. In particular, we need to know more about the total economic value of wetlands which will be lost if wetlands are destroyed, especially if this destruction proves to be irreversible.

ECONOMIC IMPORTANCE OF WETLANDS

Given the significance of previous wetland losses, and given society's desire to achieve sustainable economic development, it is clear that a balance will have to be struck between wetland degradation and economic growth. Striking this balance will require some sort of management process. But this process will not be costless. In order to determine whether or not these costs are worth the investment, we will inevitably have to assess the values of the services provided by wetlands.

The wide range of potential functions and services provided by conserved wetlands is indicated in Table 1.1 (right hand column). The interaction between wetland hydrology and topology, soil saturation, and emergent vegetation, more or less determines the general characteristics and the significance of the physical processes that occur in a given wetland. These processes are subsequently responsible for the functional services which produce *indirect use values*. Ecosystem structure (*i.e.* tangible items, such as plants, animals, soil, air and water) yields *structural* benefits of *direct use value* to humans (commercial products, recreation, aesthetic appreciation, scientific research and education value), as well as so-called *non-use values*.

To summarize, wetlands provide flood water storage, important wildlife habitats, nutrient cycling/storage and related pollution control, landscape and amenity services, recreational services, non-use existence value benefits, agricultural output, other commercial output, shoreline protection and buffer zones, and extended food web control. In short, it is easy to demonstrate the multifunctionality of wetlands.

It is also important to point out that the contributions of wetlands extend beyond the boundaries of the wetland itself, and for some classes of wetland may be globally significant. For example, wetlands often support migratory fish and bird populations of international importance. It was this latter aspect of wetland values that led to the establishment of the Ramsar Convention.

Spanish wetlands, for example, are key parts of the migratory routes of several million waterfowl birds of the Western Palearctic. Some 42 per cent of the waterfowl using these areas (95 species) are endangered species. Many rare or endangered species of animals and plants also exist permanently in these wetlands.

Organic-soil wetlands, under natural conditions, may also operate as net carbon sinks (Armentano and Menges, 1986). Functionally, some scientists argue that wetlands are important links in the global cycling of carbon dioxide and other atmospheric gases. Drainage of these peatlands and their exploitation via peat extraction may have contributed to global shifts in the balance of carbon movement between the wetlands and the atmosphere over the last two centuries. Many wetlands may also be net carbon sources, leading to increased CO_2 releases to the atmosphere. This represents a contribution (probably not significantly large) to potential global warming, and consequent damage to, among other assets, coastal wetlands!

Some scientific uncertainties still surround the precise extent and significance of the full range of wetland functions and services, so it is not possible to accurately calculate the marginal product (in economic terms) of any given wetland acreage. There is also significant uncertainty about the potential aggregate role that the remaining global wetlands stock may play in the biosphere. Enough evidence is available, however, to demonstrate that wetlands are important ecosystems which will often yield significant structural and functional benefits, if kept in a conserved state.

In other words, we can speak of a wetland infrastructure which possesses significant *total economic value,* which is not restricted only to direct use value. These ecosystems also provide substantial indirect use values, *i.e.* the indirect support and protection provided to economic activity and property by the wetland's natural functions. These are known as "environmental services". The OECD case studies emphasise that only actual "use" values (direct, and some indirect uses), such as agricultural and other commercial outputs, recreation, flood protection and storm buffer functions, are readily measurable in monetary terms via market (or proxy market) prices. Nevertheless, the environmental economics literature suggests that "non-use" values (*e.g.* option and existence values) may be significant (in terms of peoples' willingness to pay) for a wide range of environmental resources, such as wetlands.

Environmental economists have therefore gone a considerable way towards a taxonomy of *economic values* as they relate to natural environments. The terminology is still not fully agreed, but the approach is based on the traditional explanation of how value occurs, *i.e.* it is based on the interaction between a human subject (the valuer) and objects (things to be valued). Individuals have a number of "held" values, which in turn result in objects being assigned various values.

In order to arrive at a measure of total economic value, economists begin by distinguishing user values from intrinsic values. In a straightforward sense, user values derive from the actual use of the environment. Slightly more complex are those values expressed as options to continue to use the environment (*option values*). These are essentially expressions of prefer-ence (willingness to pay) for the preservation of an environment against some probability that the individual will make use of it at a later date. Provided the uncertainty concerning this future use is an uncertainty relating to the "supply" of the environment, economic theory indicates that this option value is likely to be positive. A related form of value is *bequest value* – a willingness to pay to preserve the environment for the benefit of one's children and grandchildren.

Intrinsic values present more problems. They suggest values which are in the real nature of the thing but unassociated with actual use, or even the option to use the thing. Instead such values are taken to be entities that reflect people's preferences, but include concern for, sympathy with, respect for the rights or welfare of non-human beings. Individuals may value the very existence of certain species or whole ecosystems (*existence value*). *Total economic value is then made up of actual use value + option value + existence value.*

Some progress has been made by economists attempting to determine empirical (mone-tary) measures of both environmental "use" and "non-use" values. None of the available valuation techniques (see next section) are problem free, but enough empirical work has been done to indicate that humans *do* value the environment positively. Interestingly, non-use values appear to be significantly positive. While the estimates made so far are subject to quite wide error margins, no-one can doubt that the values uncovered are real and important (Pearce and Turner, 1990).

The social benefit of wetland conservation is the total economic value (TEV) of the conserved asset. The social cost of wetlands conservation is the forgone values from non-conservation uses. The change in the TEV as the amount of the conserved asset is varied is the "shadow price" of the asset. If the shadow price deviates from the market price, it may be necessary to "correct" the market price by using economic instruments.

Given the wide range of services provided by wetlands, and the difficulty of expressing the value of some of these services in monetary terms, it seems reasonable to assume that the real total value of wetlands in OECD countries is much higher than has usually been assumed.

It then follows that wetlands have probably not been managed in an economically efficient way, because resource users have lacked appropriate economic signals which reflect the full social costs and benefits of this resource utilisation. In these circumstances, overutilisation (often leading to complete wetland destruction) of the total resource stock is inevitable.

The precise factors accounting for the overuse of wetlands are examined in more detail below. But there seems little doubt that any radical alteration and intensive utilisation of the remaining wetlands stock will result in a significant net loss of social value.

The significance of any given wetland's structural/functional benefit will vary according to its "context", or to its geographic setting. Thus location, regional scarcity of the wetland type, and national/regional culture, will (among other factors) all influence the type and magnitude of a given wetland's benefit value.

A strong *qualitative* case has now been made in support of the proposition that wetlands are valuable resources, which if retained in a conserved state, will yield significant total economic value. But what progress has been made by economists attempting to *quantify* the value of wetlands in monetary terms? It is to this question that we now turn.

ECONOMIC VALUATION METHODS AND TECHNIQUES

Standard economic methodologies exist for measuring the loss of social welfare associated with inefficient resource use (*i.e.* degradation or destruction of that part of the remaining wetlands stock for which suitable substitutes do not exist). But, especially for some indirect wetland benefits (and, in practice, for non-use values), non-monetary data will also be required to aid the decision process.

In the case of the most valuable wetlands (complex wetlands of international or national significance on the basis of being prime or scarce habitats for migratory species; unique or rare and irreplaceable ecosystems or scenic landscapes; critical habitats for endangered or threatened species; and providers of valuable functional services for the economy, such as storm buffers and flood protection zones); the lack of substitution possibilities; and the presence of scientific and other uncertainties implies that economic development via wetland conversion is often an irreversible policy decision. In these cases, the economic decision should, more often than not, simply be to *not* convert the wetland.

For those development activities that result in temporary water quality degradation and localised wetland damages, some mitigation measures (*e.g.* new institutional rules governing recreation activities or waste discharges) may be available, and the damages may be reversible, albeit at a cost.

In the case of relatively less valuable wetlands (wetlands of regional or local significance on the basis of, being valuable habitats which may be becoming scarce for fish and wildlife, or useful abundant habitats; regionally or locally uncommon ecosystems or scenic landscapes; and providers of functional services important to the regional or local economy, *e.g.* flood protection and wastewater effluent sink services), some substitution possibilities may exist, and the original wetland conversion/degradation decision may be at least partially reversible.

Mitigation may take the form of off-site measures, such as conserving and/or restoring similar wetlands elsewhere in the region; reconstructing artificial wetlands; or transferring wetland habitats to new sites. On-site measures, such as new usage rules or new conservation strategies, may also be available. If the sustainable management approach is adhered to, such compensating offsets (shadow projects) for wetland conversion or degradation should be fully costed, and added to the wetland development project costs in an extended cost-benefit appraisal.

Whether or not these mitigation (compensating offset) measures represent sufficient "compensation" for lost wetlands is a moot point. Given some degree of irreversibility and uncertainty, economics instructs the decision-maker to be cautious. This stricture is especially relevant if it is believed that the total remaining stock of wetlands is already below some definable safe minimum standard.

Table 1.2 and Figure 1.2 list the different components of the total economic value of wetlands, and the techniques available, in principle, to quantify the monetary measure of such benefits. They also indicate some of the relevant empirical studies that have been undertaken to date.

Market prices have traditionally been used to value natural wetlands as a habitat for commercially-harvested fish and animal species. Analytically, the problem is to determine the marginal productivity of an acre of wetland net of any human effort effect. Studies estimating the value of coastal marshes in the United States have come up with a wide range of monetary

Table 1.2. **Valuation of Wetland Structure and Functions**

Type of Benefit	Economic Valuation Techniques	Studies Reported in the Literature
Direct OutputBenefits (goods/services) Commercial and sport fishery; furs; recreation.	Public prices; marginal productivity value; market pricing; participation models with unit-day recreational values; hedonic pricing; travel cost models; contingent valuation.	Lynne *et al.* (1981); Batie & Wilson (1979); Gupta & Foster (1975); Park & Batie (1979); Costanza *et al.* (1987) and (1989); Mendelsohn *et al.* (1983); Thibodeau & Ostro (1981); Brown & Pollakowski (1977); Bishop & Heberlein (1980); and Farber & Costanza (1987).
Indirect Functional Benefits (flood control; groundwater recharge; waste treatment; atmospheric and life-support functions.	Damage cost avoided analysis; alternative/substitute costs; energy analysis.	Gosselink *et al.* (1974); Costanza *et al.* (1987) and (1989); Gupta & Foster (1975); Tchobanoglous & Culp (1980); Fritz & Helle (1979); Williams (1980); Thibodeau & Ostro (1981); Kahn & Kemp (1985); Farber & Costanza (1987).
Option and Non-use Value	Contingent valuation.	
Foregone Development Output Value (agricultural output; recreational housing).	Opportunity cost models	Turner *et al.* (1983); Batie & Shabman (1982); Shabman *et al.* (1979); Batie & Mabbs-Zeno (1985); Shabman & Bertlesen (1979); Turner (1988); and Bowers (1983).

Figure 1.2. **Wetland benefits valuation**

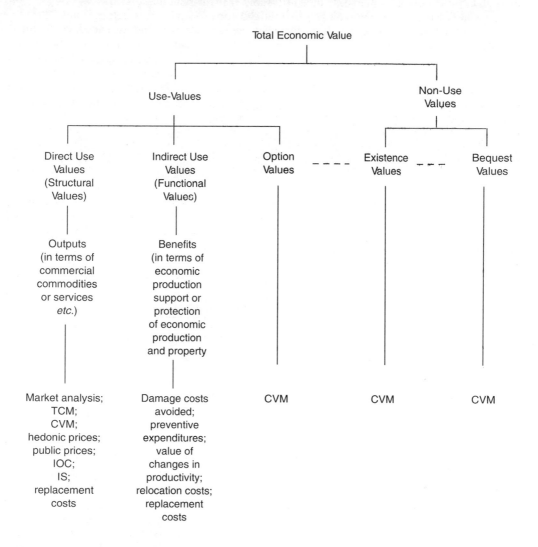

marginal product and productivity figures; from $0.30 per acre (1981 prices) to $25.36 per acre per year (1983 prices) for shellfish and fish output.

Attempts have also been made in the USA to estimate the wildlife and visual-cultural benefits of wetlands, using market land prices as indicators of the opportunity cost of wetland preservation (Gupta and Foster, 1975). The economic benefits of these two service flows were implicitly derived from the prices paid by public agencies to purchase wetlands for conservation purposes, with due regard for the natural attributes of the land. Data on more than 8 000 acres of wetlands acquired by public agencies was analysed, and a figure of $1 200 per acre was selected as representative of the capitalised value of wildlife benefits from the 'highest quality' land. The capital value of the "highest quality" open-space land was estimated to be $5 000 per acre. Prices for lower grades of land were obtained by scaling to "expert" quality-scoring indexes developed by ecologists and landscape architects. The main analytical weakness of this type of analysis is that consumer surplus is not generally estimated. Therefore, the benefits are underestimated by the amount of consumer surplus that *does* exist.

The *hedonic pricing* approach requires data on, and makes a number of assumptions about household mobility and informational requirements, as well as about the operation of the residential property market. Analysts using this method attempt to estimate the first-stage marginal (implicit) price function for proximity to water, and for water-related open space (defined in the United States as a "setback"). In one such study (Brown and Pollakowski, 1977), sample areas were all located close to one of three lakes within the Seattle (USA) city limits. The data used consisted of market sales information for dwelling units in these areas over the period 1969-74. The results suggested that variations in setbacks *did* have a substantial effect on property sales values.

Other US analysts have tried to construct an index of attribute factors to value coastal waterfront land. For example, data for land sales in Virginia Beach, Virginia, over the period 1953-76, have been used to empirically estimate a hedonic price equation. Again, it was found that an increased level of amenity gave increased values and that, over time, the annual value of the amenity increases (Shabman and Bertelsen, 1979).

However, the hedonic price approach can, at best, only capture part of the aggregate wetland value. Take, for example, the limiting case of a remote and unique wetland site threatened by mining development or pollution. The absence of local residents – as opposed to recreationists – would preclude the use of either wage or property data. Furthermore, the scenic vistas and other elements of the site are unique. And finally, non-use values are not, of course, being captured by this method.

Debate continues over the question of whether or not hedonic pricing models have successfully made the jump from an estimated property value/environmental quality gradient to actual willingness-to-pay functions. Milon *et al.* (1984) have also recently noted that, although reported coefficients for water amenity-related variables in published hedonic pricing studies generally had the expected sign, a number of different functional forms were used to describe the amenity relationship. They suggested that there is considerable reason for concern about the choice of functional form.

Wetlands have significant value as recreational areas, and three valuation techniques (participation models, travel cost methods and contingent valuation methods) have been deployed in order to capture this aspect of the ecosystem service.

A *participation model,* based on national unit-day values of recreational activities undertaken in the Charles River wetlands near Boston (USA) has been used to value five types of recreation activity. The results ranged from $32 to $102 per acre/year (Thibodeau and Ostro, 1981).

The limitations of the participation model approach include the lack of meaningful coefficients linking water quality and recreational activity, as well as the artificiality of the "recreation day value". It is doubtful whether the latter represents an adequate estimation of the value of recreation sites to the average user.

Travel cost methods (in which travel costs are taken as surrogates for visit market prices) have been applied in cases where natural wetlands provide recreation services.

The travel cost method works best when visitors travel from a wide range of distances to a wetland site, and when they only visit that one site. The method has been criticised on a number of grounds (both theoretical and empirical). These include the assumptions required about the value of time and time costs; the existance of congestion and quality deterioration; and the "weak complementarity" assumption which precludes non-use value. One recent example of this approach (see Costanza, Farber, and Maxwell, 1987; Farber, 1988; and Costanza and Farber, 1989) involved a survey of recreationists using wetlands in Terrebonne Parish, Louisiana, over a period of a year. The value of travel time was expressed in terms of a cost of travel time quantified via foregone wages. The typical user group (2.72 persons) was estimated to forego average total hourly wages of $26.90. Annual total willingness to pay using this approach ranged between $2 million and $5 million. The willingness-to-pay results are, however, questionable, because the number of visitors who were non-local was quite small.

Another travel cost study (Bishop and Heberlein, 1980) examined the value of goose hunting in the Horicon Marsh area of central Wisconsin during 1978. Using the traditional zonal variant of the travel cost method, this study found individual willingness-to-pay estimates ranging from $8 to $32, depending upon whether travel time and time at the site were included.

Because the travel cost method can only capture recreation values, it is fair to conclude that the method is not adequate as an estimator of total wetland conservation value. Wetlands are not homogeneous resources. Structural and functional characteristics vary, to some extent, and certainly from type to type. Non-use values from wetlands cannot be captured by the travel cost method.

Contingent valuation methods, defined as "any approach to valuation of a commodity which relies upon individual responses to contingent circumstances posited in an artificially structured market" (Seller *et al.* 1985) have proved popular in recent years. The results of a simulated market method and a contingent valuation method (administered via a mail questionnaire) have recently been compared, in order to estimate the recreational value (duck hunting) of Horicon Marsh, Wisconsin. It was found that the contingent valuation method yielded a willingness-to-pay of $21, as against a simulated market value of $63. (Bishop and Heberlein, 1980).

In principle, the contingent valuation approach can be used to capture all the components of total economic value, including non-use (existence) value. In practice, there have not yet been any published contingent valuation studies which incorporate non-use wetland value estimates.

Overall, too little attention has so far been paid to the question of the comparative validity of estimates of recreational value, derived from alternative valuation methods under similar conditions or problem settings. Encouragingly, when two contingent valuation models (close-ended and open-ended question format) and a travel cost valuation model (regional model) were compared in 1985 in the context of recreational boating on freshwater in the Four Lakes region of Texas, it was found that the close-ended form of the contingent valuation method and the travel cost method provided comparable estimates of consumers' surplus for some (but not all) of the lake sites studied (see Table 1.3).

21

Table 1.3.   **Comparison of Average Consumer's Surplus Estimates
for the Four Lakes Region, Texas**

Lake	Travel Cost ($/acre)	Contingent Valuation ($/acre)
Control	32.06	39.38
Livingstone	102.09	35.21
Houston	13.01	13.81

Source: Adapted from Seller *et al.* (1985).

Given the difficulties inherent in this validation context, it seems reasonable to recommend that at least a "second best" validation procedure should be adopted. In other words, the results from alternative valuation method should be compared for approximate consistency under similar conditions or problem settings. Only then can the analyst be reasonably sure that derived monetary values are in the right "ball-park" range.

Alternative/substitute cost approaches have also been used to value the indirect benefit of wetlands as municipal water supply sources. For example, the cost of delivering water from a wetland wellhead was estimated to be 0.773 cents per 1 000 gallons per day cheaper than the alternative supply source. The estimated capitalised value of a 10-acre wetland supplying one million gallons of water a day was $52 per acre, on the basis of annual benefits of $2 800 per acre (Gupta and Foster, 1975). This same approach has also been used to value the water supply benefits supplied by the Charles River wetlands in Massachusetts. The results worked out to a daily saving of $16.56 per acre, or $6 044 per acre per year ($100 730 present value, at a 6 per cent discount rate, per acre). (Thibodeau and Ostro, 1981).

Houghton Lake Marsh in Michigan has been tested (Williams, 1980) as a waste-water treatment facility over two irrigation seasons (four to six months long). In 1978-79, some 85 million gallons of effluent were applied to the 500-acre peat marsh. It is claimed that this natural facility saved more than one million dollars, as compared with the construction of an upland spray irrigation facility. Substantial operation and maintenance cost savings had an annual present value of $16 960 (at a 6 per cent discount rate).

The validity of the "alternative cost" approach depends critically on the satisfaction of three basic conditions:

1. That substitutes can provide functions or services similar to the natural wetland;
2. That the alternative chosen and costed is actually the least-cost alternative;
3. That willingness-to-pay evidence indicates that per capita demand for services would be the same at the two different levels of cost.

In Massachusetts, the US Army Corps of Engineers has compared the Charles River, a stream of relatively slow run-off and extensive wetlands, with the Blackstone River, which is characterised by rapid run-off. In a 1955 flood event, nearly 60 per cent of the flood volume passed a point on the Blackstone, while at a comparable point on the Charles, only 10 per cent passed in two days. The wetlands of the Charles River are estimated to have reduced the peak river flows by 65 per cent, and desynchronised the peak hours from the storm itself by three days.

The value of this wetland function could be interpreted in terms of the cost of the property damage which would occur if the wetlands were lost, *i.e.* on the *damage costs avoided principle*. The Corps predicted the annual monetary loss at various amounts of reduction in wetland storage. Thus, a 10 per cent wetland loss produced annual property losses of $707 000, while a 40 per cent loss produced damages of $3 192 000. Other analysts have predicted that the total loss of the Charles River wetlands would increase flood damage costs by $17 million, some $2 000 per acre of wetland (present value of $33 000, at a 6 per cent discount rate) (Thibodeau and Ostro, 1981).

In some regions, marshes also offer protection from tidal surges and wind velocities in storms. It has been calculated (Costanza and Farber, 1989) that if the Terrebonne wetlands in Louisiana receded by one mile, expected flood damages in a four-parish area would increase by $5 752 816 annually. The loss of a one-acre strip running the length of the Terrebonne Parish coastline would increase expected damages by $128.30 per acre annually (present value equal to $71 910 200, at an 8 per cent discount rate for the one mile strip, and $1 604 for one acre). If it is assumed that population grows at 1.3 per cent annually, the present value of the damages would be $1 915 per acre, or $85 900 000 in total. If the wetlands were allowed to recede at their present rate, increased property damage would have a present value of between $2 136 092 and $3 133 440.

A number of estuarine and delta wetlands have been heavily polluted by upstream agricultural and industrial activities. One recent study (Kahn and Kemp, 1985) tried to establish a lower bound of the marginal damage function for reductions in the level of submerged aquatic vegetation in Chesapeake Bay, USA. The loss of the vegetation, due to nutrient enrichment, would have an adverse impact on the wetland fisheries. A 20 per cent reduction in the vegetation results in estimated total annual losses for finfish and shellfish of approximately $1 million (1978 prices). The total loss of vegetation would produce fisheries damage costs of $13 to $14 million. These estimates are only lower bound figures because no account is taken of damage to waterfowl, hunting, bird watching and other recreational activities. Since the Bay represents a unique and important ecosystem, existence values are also likely to be quite large.

The opportunity cost approach represents a pragmatic perspective on the valuation dilemma, without itself being a valuation technique. Thus, the opportunity cost of unpriced wetland functions and services can be estimated from the foregone income of potential development uses. So the costs of conserving the wetland can be put into context indirectly, by assessing the opportunity costs involved (*i.e.* the foregone social net benefits of the development activity, drainage scheme, afforestation programme, *etc.*). For example, many of the agricultural improvement schemes (involving drainage and flood alleviation components) undertaken during the 1970s and early 1980s in the United Kingdom have been critically reassessed. Analysts have argued that the true social costs of conservation (of a range of wetlands) were not especially high, and that the conservation option may even have represented a net benefit (Bowers, 1983 and 1988; Turner, Dent & Hey, 1983). For example, the legitimate economic costs of conservation are those of foregone agricultural output value, but *minus* the value of any agricultural protection policies, such as capital grants and price supports.

Estimating the precise social value of foregone agricultural outputs in Europe is complicated by the budgetary flows involved in the CAP system. Two basic methods have been suggested for calculating the social cost of the foregone agricultural output – the Producer Subsidy Equivalents (PSE) method, and the Effective Protection Rate (EPR) method (Willis, Benson & Saunders, 1988). The subsidy element varies from year to year and from crop to crop. The PSE method yields higher subsidy estimates than the EPR, but over a period of years, there is no doubt that many crop prices where intervention occurred were well above world market prices. As of 1988/89, the UK MAFF recommended a 20 per cent value reduction for both beef and cereals output, to take account of the implicit subsidy element.

A recent analysis of the social benefit to be gained by improving agriculture in three selected environmentally significant areas (one was a wetland) found them to be positive. Thus, for these particular sites, there is a social cost involved in the conservation option. However, even though restrictions on agriculture may involve a social cost, this social cost is nevertheless only a fraction of the financial cost involved. Without the CAP, the amount of compensation required (assuming free trade in agricultural commodities) to compensate farmers for restrictions on agricultural outputs on significant sites could be considerably less than that under the present financial guidelines for management agreements outlined by the UK Department of the Environment in 1983 (Willis & Benson, 1988; Willis, Benson & Saunders, 1988).

In the United States, the opportunity costs of conserving coastal wetland sites have also been quantified (Batie & Mabbs-Zeno, 1985). Results indicate that, in several cases, the "conservation of wetlands" option does not involve significantly high social costs.

Two of the major pressures for the development of Virginia's wetlands, for example, have been for residential home development in urbanising coastal areas, and for water access (marinas) and recreation home development in the more rural areas of the state. Two studies undertaken in the 1970s used a hedonic price equation in order to regress land sale prices on a set of explanatory variables representing individual land unit characteristics. The characteristics included measures of water access and waterfront location created from filled wetlands (Shabman et al., 1979).

In Virginia Beach (an area already under heavy development pressures, and therefore possessing high marginal preservation values), the opportunity costs of conservation, if development is designed for residential units, are *not* particularly high. These gross benefit estimates have to be further reduced by the development costs which would be necessary to fill in and develop the wetlands. In Captain's Cove (located in a rural area), five acres of marsh were initially destroyed to construct a marina and common recreation area. This marina provided water access to 3 700 interior land units. The development benefits depend crucially on whether so-called "fastland sites" are available as alternative development options. The marina had a marginal value of $5 800 per acre, but subsequent wetland losses to provide housing produced only minor benefits (of $37 per acre).

These results all assume that no fastland alternative site is available. When a fastland alternative location that provides water access *is* available without necessitating wetland losses, and is used as the next best alternative for comparison, net wetland development values are only positive when large areas of marsh are converted.

The opportunity cost approach does illustrate that estimates of wetland development benefits can provide a focus for an application of a *safe minimum standard* rule, or a *no net-loss* rule for wetland conservation. It is also in line with an argument made earlier that, given the general, on-going loss of wetlands, and the uncertainties surrounding the precise magnitude and significance of wetlands services/functions, wetland developers should have to positively demonstrate the net social benefits of their actions, rather than *vice versa*. The use of alternative development values has great utility in this uncertain policy context.

Evidence from all the OECD case studies confirms the general proposition that wetland resources have not always been managed efficiently in the past, and in some areas continue to be overexploited. The next section of the report contains an analysis of the *sources* of this problem of inefficient wetland utilisation.

MARKET AND INTERVENTION FAILURES IN OECD WETLANDS

The overutilisation of the total wetlands stock has been the result of a combination of:

- *"Natural" land use conflicts,* largely due to the attractive spatial location (*i.e.* on level terrain, often with highly productive soils and easy access). These factors combine to make wetlands attractive for a diverse range of competing economic activities. Over time, many wetland sites have therefore been lost, as economies have industrialised and their agricultural sectors have become more intensive. Much of this historical loss does not represent inefficient resource usage in itself, but some damages have been caused by "failure" factors;
- *Information failures* (*i.e.* a general lack of appreciation of the full economic value of conserved wetlands), which has in turn contributed to both market and intervention failure;
- *Market failures* (in particular wetlands have suffered, to a greater or lesser extent, from pollution [an externality problem]; and from surface water or ground water supply diminution as a result of excessive abstraction of open-access water resources [public good failure]). It is also the case that most of the benefits of wetland services do not accrue to the wetland owner himself, so there is a divergence between private and social benefits; and
- *Intervention failure* (the general absence of nationally-integrated resource management policy has resulted in intersectoral policy inconsistencies, leading to wetland destruction/degradation. There are also examples of inefficient policies directed at wetlands themselves and policies directed at other sectoral issues which carry with them unintended/inadvertent spillover effects for wetlands).

Natural land use conflicts, largely because of multiple-use pressures, have afflicted coastal and estuarine wetlands to a greater extent than other wetland types. Agricultural reclamation, urban and industrial development, and recreational pressures have all contributed to the substantial loss of these coastal and estuarine wetlands.

The most ubiquitous form of *market failure* encountered during the case studies was "externalities". All types of wetlands have suffered, to a greater or lesser extent, from externalities that have resulted in pollution damage (both on- and off-site pollution sources). Industrial and agricultural pollution (in some instances, combined with sewerage effluent) have served in subtle and complicated ways to degrade wetlands (both chemically and biologically). In the majority of cases, water-borne pollution has been the main problem, but some upland wetlands have also suffered degradation because of air pollution in the form of acid deposition. The degradation process usually results in a series of latent impacts, including loss of species diversity. Saltmarshes, coastal marshes and intertidal mudflats are also all at risk from climate change-induced sea level rise.

The run-off of agricultural chemicals and soil erosion (increased sedimentation) have combined with point-source pollution from effluent treatment plants to inflict serious damage on estuarine wetlands, such as in Chesapeake Bay (USA). Similar environmental impacts have been felt in the Norfolk Broadlands in the United Kingdom, and elsewhere in Europe. Other wetlands have been degraded by industrial effluent discharge to watercourses which subsequently flow through, or near wetlands. The Po delta wetlands in Italy, for example, have been heavily polluted and degraded by industrial effluent.

Because these pollution-induced biological and chemical changes in wetlands are often latent impacts, and do not, in the short run, result in obvious physical changes, they pose significant management problems. It may also be the case that most estimates of wetland loss underestimate the true rate of on-going wetland degradation, because they are limited to the observation of physical changes. This on-going rate of loss will require more than just the cessation of new activities to offset it.

In regions which possess relatively dry climates, wetlands have been damaged because they possess some of the characteristics of public goods (*i.e.* non-exclusion or prohibitively expensive exclusion of potential resource users). This "open-access" situation has led to reductions in the amount surface water supplied to wetlands, as well as to groundwater supply depletion. For example, in the Daimiel National Park, as well as the Laguna de las Salinas and the Laguna de la Celadilla wetlands in Spain, continuous exploitation of a limited source of water (mainly for irrigated agriculture) has led to surface drying in wetland areas, and fears that the entire groundwater aquifer resource is itself being depleted.

The conservation value (particularly the non-use value) of wetlands is also a public or quasi-public good (non-exclusion and non-rivalry in usage, for both current users and potential future users). Thus, we need to take into account the potentially significant *option* and *existence* values. Failure to account for such values may represent a failure to meet an intergenerational efficiency objective. If the infilling of wetlands represents their permanent removal, this may represent a denial of an opportunity for future generations to benefit from wetland services.

From the wetlands resource management viewpoint, the key factor is that in the presence of such "publicness", markets will undersupply wetland conservation (environmental value) benefits. Again, the need for policy intervention mechanisms is highlighted.

Where wetlands supply recreational opportunities, these goods/services are examples of "congestible" goods. There is the danger that utilisation levels might result in overcrowding and subsequent declines in resource quality, as the wetland's "carrying capacity" is exceeded. In the case of "congestible" goods, exclusion results in efficient use only if consumers pay for their use in accordance with their willingness to pay. There are, however, usually obstacles (*e.g.* high transaction costs) both to collecting such payments and to eliciting their true (full) valuations. Nevertheless, some exclusion-type management devices are possible. For example, in the Norfolk Broads (UK), recreation pressure (in terms of boating activities) is regulated to some extent by limits on the number of boat licences issued for hire craft.

The absence of property rights means that farmers, for example, have little incentive to protect wetland values against actions that would diminish their supply, or to take actions that would increase their supply in response to expected future increases in demand. In the case of wetland services, such property rights are poorly developed (or absent altogether), essentially because of a lack of control of access to the wetland service, or because the value of this service is less than the cost of controlling access to it.

The *intervention failure* category is a complicated one and, in some cases, is linked to both information and market failures. It should also be recognised that it is sometimes difficult to say conclusively what constitutes an intervention failure. Historically, a large number of wetland conversions in developed economies probably did represent socially beneficial resource allocation decisions. These conversions, for example, often led to much-needed agricultural output, and to reduced threats to human health. The same general argument is probably applicable to some wetland conversions in the contemporary developing economies.

Nevertheless, there are several examples of socially inefficient policies, often specifically directed at wetlands. The Spanish Water Act of 1879 (valid until 1985) included a provision which classified lagoons and shallow- water environments as "unhealthy areas". Tax deductions and other economic incentives were made available to encourage the drainage and reclamation of such areas – especially in the period after 1950. But this policy had the effect of classifying all wetlands as "unhealthy", and therefore stimulated an inefficient (excess) level of wetland conversion.

Some policies attempting to foster the sustainable usage of wetlands have proved to be inefficient because they lacked a long enough time horizon. Thus, the introduction of relatively low-intensity fishfarming in some French wetlands initially served to keep the wetlands and their reedbeds intact. But new technology for reed cutting, and subsidies for intensive fishfarming, now pose a threat to the long-term survival of the wetlands.

Developing countries too have suffered from inefficient wetland policies. In peninsular Malaysia, for example, many freshwater swamps have been drained for rice cultivation. But yields have been disappointing because the fields have lacked a regular supply of freshwater. This water was traditionally supplied by the swamps. Overall, in developed and developing economies, sustainable development represents a fragile balance between technology, economics and environmental conservation.

The absence of nationally-integrated resource management policies has also resulted in many intervention failures in both developed and developing countries. These failures take the form of intersectoral policy inconsistencies, which lead to wetland destruction or degradation. The interface between agricultural conversion and intensification policies on the one hand, and wetland (especially lowland freshwater types) conservation on the other, is the most ubiquitous example of this variant of intervention failure.

Saline soil marshes in the United Kingdom, France and Holland and interior wetlands (northern prairie potholes and southern bottomland hardwood forested wetlands) in North America have suffered particularly high losses, due to conversion to high-intensity agriculture. The agricultural conversion processes have been artificially stimulated by a range of subsidies, price guarantees, and tax incentives given to farmers.

In the United States, it is necessary to distinguish between the situation which existed prior to the passage of a new Farm Bill in 1985 (with its "swampbuster" provision), and more recent years. Before 1985, drainage subsidies had the effect of expanding the output of agricultural commodities already in oversupply (for which the government was sometimes granting other subsidies to *discourage* this condition). In other words, the US government has compensated farmers who set aside croplands, in order to reduce the production of the very same crops expanded on adjacent drained wetlands whose conversion was aided by government incentives. Within the US Department of Agriculture (USDA), incentives for wetland drainage and cropland expansion were paid out of one account (Federal Crop Insurance Agency); incentives for wetland conversion out of another account (Water Bank); and yet a third mechanism provided land retirement payments to farmers to reduce crop surpluses (Payments in Kind).

While the USDA has been promoting the drainage of wetlands, the Department of the Interior has been seeking to protect them. USDA has subsidised small watershed flood control projects, including stream channelisation, which indirectly facilitates the ditching and drainage of adjacent wetlands. Local landowners have been able to drain into federally-financed channels, and then insure the crops grown on converted wetlands against flood damage and other disasters. The Interior Department, on the other hand, seeks to purchase wetlands in fee or perpetual easement for permanent conservation, including those lost to conversions aided by USDA incentives. Thus, both flood control and drainage projects encouraged by the Army

Corps of Engineers and the USDA's Soil Conservation Service have increased production from bottomland farms, as well as their market value, and reduced the risk of losses from floods.

Farmers in the United States were compensated for retiring land from the production of crops in oversupply, often the same crops grown on converted wetlands drained with public assistance. They also received income tax write-offs for drainage investments; below-market loans were available for drainage expenditure; and crop flooding insurance was available for converted wetlands.

Since the new Farm Bill of 1985, price supports, crop insurance, disaster payments and low-interest loans are now all unavailable to farmers who convert wetlands to arable cropping via drainage, excavation, filling, levelling or other means. There are some exemptions, however, such as, for example, wetlands established by irrigation run-off. Despite their non-natural origins, such wetlands may be very important to wildlife in dry-farming regions.

In Europe, farmers have also been subsidised in their efforts to drain (and convert) wetlands and traditional grazing marshes into arable cropping. In France in the past, some 10 to 60 per cent of the costs of field drainage, ditches and channels have been paid out of public funds. The UK's Ministry of Agriculture, Fisheries and Food (UK MAFF) has also (up to the mid 1980's) operated a system of drainage grants for farmers converting land to higher productivity crops.

However, the real driving force behind the conversion of wetlands in Europe has been the high general level of intervention prices paid for a number of crops under the EEC's Common Agricultural Policy. Under the CAP, intervention cereals prices have at certain times been well above world market prices (*e.g.* EEC wheat prices were 40 to 60 per cent above world market prices over the period 1978-80). The effect was to make the conversion of lowland wet grazing meadows in the United Kingdom (for winter wheat) a very profitable financial investment for individual farmers. This financial enticement, combined with public financing of arterial drainage works and government grants for field drainage have compounded the overproduction problem, and accelerated the wetland loss rate (Bowers, 1988).

UK MAFF's "departmental view" has historically been that its function is to ensure the maximum growth of agricultural output and of agricultural productivity, within the limits of the resources at its disposal. Land drainage and flood protection were seen as strategic instruments in securing those ends, and hence were subsidised. MAFF need "exercise their functions so as to further conservation", only insofar as this may be consistent with the aims of increased production. Until 1985, UK farmers had been aided in their land conversions by supporting agencies (Regional Water Authorities and local Internal Drainage Boards) who have sponsored flood protection and major arterial drainage schemes. Field drainage schemes which serve to increase farm productivity qualified for a 50 per cent grant from MAFF. Flood protection and arterial drainage works carried out by Water Authorities and Drainage Boards were also (under certain circumstances) subsidised by MAFF grants.

Another UK public agency, The Nature Conservancy Council (NCC), which is charged with a nature conservation remit, could be required to compensate farmers whose methods were required to remain unchanged in order to conserve, for example, traditional grazing marshes. Thus, while the UK Wildlife and Countryside Acts of 1981 and 1985, were designed to protect exceptional conservation assets (SSSI's and nature reserves), they are still based on voluntary codes of conduct, instead of on statutory powers and penalties to prevent the destruction of the countryside.

The 1981 Act also included provisions for the development of management agreements (between NCC and landowners) to compensate farmers when grants for conversion schemes had been refused by MAFF on conservation grounds. Farmer claims under a management agreement are based on calculations of (financial) profits foregone, due to the necessity to continue traditional low-intensity farming. Conservation policy, under this management option, is very expensive in financial terms.

A number of other intersectoral policy inconsistency situations involving wetlands can be readily illustrated:

a) Energy policy involving peat extraction in Northern Europe, and the associated loss of peat bog wetlands;
b) Other resource extraction policies, involving phosphates, coal, sand and gravel, and wetland loss;
c) Forestry policy and the destruction of blanket bogs in the United Kingdom. Globally-scarce blanket bog is found extensively in Caithness and Sutherland in Scotland. This area is now under severe threat from coniferous afforestation;
d) Recreational housing and related facilities, as well as industrial/port facilities, which have impinged on a number of coastal wetlands, both in Europe and in the United States;
e) Flood protection and navigation improvement policies involving dredging, stream channelisation, ditching and flood-banking have led to wetland loss;

Table 1.4. **A Typology of Major Types of Market and Intervention Failures**

Type of Failure	Source of Failure
1. Pollution Externalities	
a) Air pollution, off-site	Excess levels of sulphur and nitrogen, causing loss of species diversity.
b) Water pollution, on-site	Excess nitrogen and phosphorous from sewerage and agricultural sources: some industrial (toxic) pollution.
c) Water pollution, off-site	Agricultural and recreational pressures.
2. Public Goods-type Problems	
a) Ground-water depletion	Overexploitation (on- and off-site) of surface and ground water supplies, leading to the diminution of wetland water supplies.
b) Congestion costs, on-site	Recreation pressure on wetland carrying capacities.
3. Intersectoral Policy Inconsistencies	
a) Competing sector output prices	Agricultural price-fixing and subsequent land requirements.
b) Competing sector input prices	Tax breaks or outmoded tax categories on agricultural land; tax breaks for housing or industrial usage; tax breaks on forestry capital; low interest loans to farmers; conversion subsidies (drainage, fill, flood protection, flood insurance); subsidies on other agricultural inputs; and research and development biased towards intensive farming methods.
c) Land use policy	Zoning; regional development policies; direct policies favouring conversion of wetlands; agricultural set-aside schemes; waste disposal policies.
4. Counterproductive Wetlands Policies	
a) Inefficient policy	Policies that lack a long-term structure.
b) Institutional failure	Lack of monitoring and survey capacity, poor information dissemination; non-integrative agency structures.

f) Dams for water storage and hydroelectric power generators can lead to wetland destruction (*e.g.* the S. Hainberg riverine forest wetland controversy in Austria, and the loss of a number of wetlands in France);

g) Use of wetlands as waste disposal sites;

h) Regional development policies in the European Community have led (in both France and Greece) to the establishment of intensive fishfarming enterprises. These activities have sometimes polluted the surrounding wetlands and led to the abandonment of traditional (sustainable) management activities in these wetlands.

The destruction of blanket bogs in the United Kingdom offers a particularly interesting example of intervention failure. The UK Forestry Commission had been established in 1919 to rectify Britain's extreme dependency on external timber sources, which far exceeded that of other industrial economies. Since 1950, most of the afforestation programmes have been concentrated in Scotland, and to a more limited extent, in upland Wales and the North of England. Between 1979 and 1985, private afforestation also expanded rapidly in Scotland. This private expansion has been stimulated by grants and favourable tax treatment. In this situation, the development costs of the plantation can be offset against tax liabilities. This has attracted both higher-income taxpayers, and institutions to invest in forestry, with resulting pressure being placed on the bogs. (Changes to this tax policy were, however, introduced in the April 1988 budget).

In some of these situations, it is true that the impacts on the wetland have only been unintended/inadvertent spillover effects. For example, the Spanish Port Act of 1928, the Shores Act of 1969 and the Coastal Protection Act of 1980 (now abolished) all inadvertently led to the loss of coastal wetlands. The loss of Mediterranean-type coastal wetlands throughout Europe suffers from this type of problem in particular.

Table 1.4 summarises the most significant intervention and market failures identified in the national case studies.

Having examined the major causes of wetland losses, the final question to be addressed is what policy measures can and should be undertaken to avoid, minimise and mitigate any further loss of wetland conservation values? Remedial measures will typically be required at both the national and international levels.

SUSTAINABLE WETLAND MANAGEMENT STRATEGIES

Following the schema set out in Figure 1.3, this section reviews the policy instruments that are available to mitigate information, market and intervention failures. In so doing, it attempts to contribute to a future sustainable wetland management strategy, as well as looking at what can be done to slow down or halt the excessive loss of wetlands.

A successful management strategy will have to be based on data indicating the value of different classes of wetland. Enough scientific information now exists to allow an in-depth functional assessment of individual wetland classes. This functional assessment should be combined with economic valuation analysis, insofar as this is practical. Data on threats to wetlands will also have to be collected. All data collected (*i.e.* on functions, values and land-use conflicts) will ideally be available on a drainage basin-wide basis.

Figure 1.3. **Substainable management of wetlands**

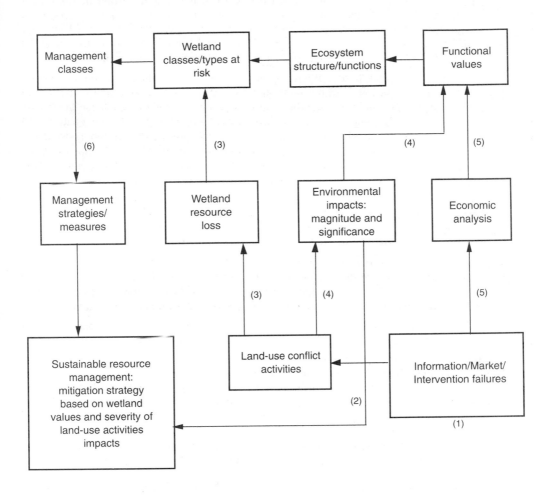

Any policy instruments package that is developed will need to be tailored to fit the particular wetlands loss context being considered.

The national case studies have served to emphasise the different ''wetland contexts'' that exist in North America (and other relatively low population density, large-land-mass economies), compared with the situation which exists in Europe. In North America, there is still an extensive network of natural and semi-natural wetlands. Therefore, the scope for ''wilderness preservation'' policies is still very high (although more limited than it was in the past). Contrast this situation with that in Europe, where most, if not all, of the wetland ecosystems and landscapes are semi-natural. Most of these wetlands have been modified, directly or indirectly, by human activities. The present-day land use pressures are also much greater in Europe than in North America.

The different physical wetland contexts between North America and Europe are reinforced by political and cultural differences. It is therefore likely that an array of policy instruments (regulatory and non-regulatory) will be required in any wetlands conservation strategy, and that the precise mix of instruments and institutions (at the national level) will vary from country to country. Table 1.5 lists the primary management measures potentially available.

In Europe, it is likely that there will have to be relatively more emphasis on policies aimed at the sustainable use of wetlands, rather than on nature reserve acquisition and conservation *per se*. In this context, sustainability must be seen as a process of balanced change guided by economic incentives and regulations (*e.g.* Environmentally Sensitive Area designation). In effect, wetlands protection strategies need to be more than just nature conservation, restricted to threatened species lists, or to the establishment of reserves. All of this is not to reject the concept of nature reserves, but to emphasise the need to buttress this policy with other options, so that as extensive a stock of wetlands as possible is retained over time.

Semi-natural wetlands can only be conserved if appropriate management rules and incentive structures can be found and retained. The challenge here is to find practicable "environmentally benign" tourist, agricultural and other commercial activities which will allow or encourage the sustainable utilisation of these wetlands.

The on-going wetland loss process in all OECD Member countries is due to a combination of market and intervention failures. The insidious problem of wetland degradation due to pollution (market failure) will require a more consistent (and probably more rigorous) application of the Polluter-Pays Principle, via pollution taxes and/or permits and/or regulations.

Greater integration in pollution control policy would also serve to enhance wetland protection. This integration can be interpreted in at least three basic ways:

  a) *Spatial integration* – non-point source pollution and cross-media pollution remain pervasive problems in all OECD economies. There is a need, therefore, to move beyond an examination of industrial plant or location-specific pollution issues, to consider impacts across a wider geographical area. Policies regulating water pollution and waste disposal, for example, can also serve to protect wetlands from chemical and biological changes;

  b) *Administrative/institutional integration* – institutional frameworks necessary to support and enable policy instruments and strategies need to cover all the environmental media;

  c) *Analytical and data integration* – the concept of "total economic value" needs to better incorporate the full functional and service values of natural capital, such as wetlands. In the practical project appraisal context, there is a need to integrate environmental impact assessment with the standard economic cost-benefit approach. Project appraisal should be seen as an on-going and anticipatory assessment process which includes all of the following stages:

    – Pre-project environmental assessment;
    – Project benefit-cost analysis;
    – Environmental impact assessment;
    – Monitoring, post-project appraisal and feedback mechanisms.

During the 1980's, several new wetland management measures were adopted in OECD Member countries. For example, in the United Kingdom, wetland loss rates have been reduced,

Table 1.5. **Wetland Management Policy Instrument Options**

Instrument		Comment
1. Regulation		
Planning designations	{ Prohibitions Zoning and designation (subject to licence/permit) Permissions	– Regulation of wetland uses and activity impact mitigation, with or without compensation. National, regional or local permits with uniform conditions.
Pollution abatement	{ Specific controls over land use (subject to licence/permit) Ambient quality standards	– Zoning and designation of wetlands by permitted use or activity; UK SSSIs, nature reserves, national/regional parks, global biospherical reserves (Ramsar Convention); varying degrees of site protection in practice.
		– Increased stringency in pollution control policy; ambient environmental.
2. Acquisition and Management		
Purchase	{ Public body Charitable body with public grant aid (covenants)	
Leasehold	Via covenant, with management	by owner by accredited agent
Management agreement	With landowner, subject to agreement	
3. Incentives and Charges		
Subsidies for conservation management	{ ESAs; management agreements Compensation for wetlands, wildlife and crop damage Conservation practices (headlands, hedgerows, *etc.*)	
Tax incentives for conservation management	{ On land On inputs and other costs	– Income, capital gains, and estate tax exemptions for protected wetlands; deductions or credits on wetland donations or sales for conservation; property tax relief for protected wetlands.
Wetland loss mitigation charges		– Wetland development fees and related public trust fund for conservation; mitigation land banks (unadulterated or restored wetlands).
User charges	{ Entrance fees Licences	– Wetland hunting, fishing licence fees; non-consumption use licences; recreation entrance fees.
Development activity subsidies	{ Agriculture Road construction Recreational Housing Forestry *etc.*	– Removal or reduction in scope/extent *e.g.* of agricultural subsidies – including drainage and irrigation cost-sharing, loans, crop flood insurance, commodity price supports; tax deductions for development costs.

due to a combination of regulatory, acquisition and management, and incentive measures. Section 28 of the Wildlife and Countryside Acts (1981-85) provides the main protective framework for environmentally valuable habitats. Conservation sites are scheduled and notified as Sites of Special Scientific Interest, under the auspices of the Nature Conservancy Council (NCC). This agency is also charged with the management of National Nature Reserves (NNR). A large number of wetlands, or parts of wetlands, are in principle protected from development because of their SSSI or NNR designation. However, in practice, this protection has sometimes proved to be inadequate, especially when development pressures have been intense.

The United Kingdom (along with all other OECD countries) is a signatory to the International Ramsar Convention, and a large number of estuarine wetlands have been designated as Ramsar Sites. Some UK estuaries and many others in Europe have also been designated as Specially Protected Areas under the European Community Directive on the Conservation of Wild Birds (EC 79/409).

UK conservation bodies have spent large sums of money on the conservation of wetlands via acquisition. This type of policy does overcome the difficulty of establishing property rights. Policies to acquire farmland of high habitat value are also in place in the United States and Canada. Both these countries have recently agreed to acquire several million acres of wetlands in the northern plains of the United States and the adjacent prairie region of Canada. Wetlands in these areas are of major importance as habitat for waterfowl, as well as for numerous other wildlife species. The basic objective of this North American Waterfowl Management Plan is to preserve some of the habitat values of these lands against further agricultural conversion.

So far, the use of public and private institutions to acquire property rights in environmentally-valuable land occurs on only a small scale relative to the total amount of land under threat of conversion (Crosson, 1990). Table 1.6 summarises the dominant types of threats posed to wetlands. It seems reasonable to conclude that land purchase alone will not be sufficient to counter the total threat to wetlands from development activities. As yet, the level of resources available to conservation bodies has only been sufficient to purchase a small proportion of the land under threat of conversion. The Canadian-American example (probably the most extensive example of the wetland purchase policy) calls for the acquisition of only five or six million acres of wetlands in an area where the total wetland acreage is in the order of tens of millions. In countries which have now lost most of their largest expanses of wetlands (*e.g.* most European countries), the purchase option also faces significant technical difficulties. Because ownership of the remaining wetland areas is frequently fragmented, the establishment of a

Table 1.6. **Spatial Location and Threats to Wetland Resources**

Wetland Types	Dominant Causes of Management Failure
1. Floodplains	Interference with hydrology; dams; river walls; rehabilitation of floodplains.
2. Coastal lagoons, river deltas, and estuaries	Land reclamation; pollution; industrial development; abstraction of water for irrigation; reduction of aquifer supply and surface waterflow; recreation pressure; hunting activities.
3. Wet meadows	Drainage schemes (on- and off-site).
4. Peatlands	Drainage schemes and agricultural reclamation; resource extraction (energy and non-energy); forestry.

viable (sizeable) wetland reserve by purchase or lease may turn out to be a very protracted process indeed.

Nevertheless, the purchase option does represent an attractive long-term wetland conservation solution. Some of the other available policy options lack this long-term perspective. Over the next few decades, policies aimed at greatly expanding purchasing activities by both public and private agencies could go a long way toward overcoming the property rights obstacles associated with increasing the ability of wetland conservation values to compete with agricultural expansion. The prospects are brightest in those countries which still retain relatively large areas of unmodified wetlands. In Europe, with its much diminished wetlands stocks, and with the heavily transformed nature of many of its remaining wetlands, the purchase option faces more difficulties. Both the fragmented nature of the wetlands stock, and the present ownership pattern of many wetland areas, complicate matters considerably.

The problem of establishing wetland reserves of an adequate size is of course complicated by the "open system" nature of wetland ecosystems. Thus, even the formal establishment of protected wetland park areas (via legislation) is only a *necessary,* rather than a *sufficient,* conservation measure for wetlands. For example, the establishment of the Coto de Doñana National Park in Spain does not incorporate the complete wetland system. Moreover, threats to the health of the wetland can originate considerable distances away from the wetland area itself (*e.g.* via air transport).

Members of the European Community all have the capability to designate "environmentally sensitive areas" (ESAs). This concept has its origin in EEC Regulation N° 797/85, introduced in March 1985, as part of a package of measures designed to mitigate the twin problems of farm income maintenance and surplus production. Under Article 19/9 of the Regulation, it is possible to recognise "areas of recognised importance from ecological and landscape points of view". Member States may make available grant-aid to farmers who undertake to farm environmentally important areas in a way that preserves or improves the environment. Regulation 797/85 is, nevertheless, primarily a means of pursuading farmers to reduce agricultural production, rather than a conservation measure *per se.*

By 1989, in the United Kingdom, some thirteen ESAs had been established, several of which (*e.g.* Broads, Somerset Levels, Suffolk River Valleys) are important wetlands. The UK ESA scheme offer financial incentives to farmers who choose to follow a set of management guidlines designed to promote traditional low-intensity land-uses. Conversion of land to arable regimes (which require deep drainage) is discouraged in favour of low-intensity summer grazing regimes (involving high water tables). In this way, both the landscape and the ecology attributes of wetlands can potentially be conserved on a sustainable use basis.

The main drawback of ESA-type schemes, as presently set up in the United Kingdom, is that the incentive payments and the reciprocal farming practices cover only a prescribed period of time (*i.e.* five years). There is a need for such schemes to be extended to cover the long-term conservation needs of wetlands.

The United States has adopted a number of different remedial measures that attempt to address both market failure and intervention failures affecting wetlands. Unfortunately, the empirical data necessary to evaluate the effectiveness of these approaches is not yet available.

Three types of regulatory programmes have been used in the United States to control wetland conversions. The first of these programmes is directed at the wetlands themselves, and generally limits or prohibits certain types of alterations of the resource.

The second type controls certain activities that may alter wetlands. For instance, a regulation that requires a hydroelectric facility to obtain a government licence before it can be built may prohibit the responsible agency from issuing the licence, when significant conversion of wetlands would result.

The third type of regulation focuses on the functional values of wetlands, particularly on their importance in providing wildlife habitat for certain species. These regulations can limit proposed alterations if they would significantly interfere with these values.

At the federal level, the only example of the first type of regulation is section 404/0 of the federal Clean Water Act. This section of the law requires anyone intending to place dredged or fill material in the waters (including most wetlands) to obtain a permit. Some States have similar regulatory programmes which are often more extensive in terms of the types of alterations they control than the section 404 programmes. Most coastal states also have planning programmes which serve to discourage wetland alterations in coastal regions. Local governments, which are usually responsible for zoning and other land use controls, may also designate wetland areas for purposes other than development.

These programmes have had some success. However, because they have been primarily restricted to regulating specific development proposals, they have probably addressed no more than 10 to 15 per cent of total wetland conversions in the United States to date.

The second type of regulatory programme (*i.e.* those covering activities that may alter wetlands) include the many programmes that require developers to obtain one or more permits from federal or state agencies before they can build their facilities or begin operations. These include hydroelectric stations, transmission lines, pipelines, mines, bridges, pollution discharges and waste disposal.

The only examples of the third regulatory approach are those programmes established to protect endangered species and migratory wildlife, (*e.g.* Endangered Species Act and the Migratory Bird Treaty).

On the non-regulatory front, the following policy measures have been adopted in the United States in an effort to protect wetlands:

    a) Public education about the benefits that wetlands provide;
    b) Tax incentives for individuals who protect wetlands;
    c) Subsidies for individuals protecting wetlands; and
    d) Public acquisition of wetland areas.

Overall, the limited experience and evidence to date points to the conclusion that market incentive measures (taxes or subsidies) will have to be combined with legislation which establishes ESAs or similar conservation zones, if extensive enough areas of wetland are to be adequately protected on a long-term basis. Some analysts have suggested that an assurance bonding system could be established in order to get prospective developers and other parties responsible for wetland loss/damage into an economic trade-off situation. The idea is that parties responsible for wetland destruction be charged the full social cost (total economic value estimate of conserved wetlands per acre) which results from their activities. These fees would go into an assurance bond to be returned to the developers in the event that damages prove to be less than the worst case estimate assumed in the original calculation of the fee. Alternatively, funds raised by the fees could be used on wetland loss mitigation schemes elsewhere in the region (Costanza, Farber & Maxwell, 1989).

Developers and/or polluters could lower future fees (or secure a return of the bond) by proving that damages were actually less than the worst case calculation, or by otherwise minimising their own impact on wetlands. There would be a strong economic incentive for these parties to seek out impact-minimisation options, as well as to fund research into the functional value of wetlands, in order to test the validity of the worst case fee calculation.

In recent years, the US government has adopted, through legislation, executive orders, and agency guidance, a number of mechanisms for reducing inadvertent wetland impacts resulting from intervention failures. This effort has also been matched at the state and local level, although generally less extensively and less aggressively.

The earliest federal law requiring agencies to assess the impact of their actions on wetlands was the National Environmental Policy Act 1969. This was later followed by the Fish and Wildlife Coordination Act and two executive orders – one pertaining to wetlands (E.O. 11990), and the second relating to floodplains (E.O. 11988). Provisions in the Water Resources Development Act of 1986 increased the amount of local cost-sharing required for water resource projects which are likely to impact on wetlands. The aim was to restrain the number and size of the project(s) undertaken. This same Act also established a Federal/State-funded Wetlands Trust to protect, enhance, restore and manage prairie pothole wetlands.

In the same year (1986) Congress enacted a "swamp buster" provision in the Food Security Act. This provision makes persons cultivating crops on wetlands converted after 23 December 1985 ineligible to receive any federal farm programme benefits. The provision does not apply sanctions to the wetlands alteration itself, but only when the converted lands are planted with crops.

Finally, the Tax Reform Act of 1986 removed several tax inducements to wetlands conversions. (It is debatable, however, whether in the US context, these incentives had ever been crucial to the original conversion decisions).

CONCLUSIONS

Evidence from all the case studies illustrates that OECD wetland loss rates have histori-cally been substantial and, in a number of instances, remain high. Precisely quantified national loss rates are not available, but there is some evidence to suggest that current estimates may still underrepresent the reality.

Market and intervention failures have been at the root of these problems in most, if not all, OECD countries. The most obvious area for concern has been the systematic conversion of wetlands to other uses, especially agricultural, industrial and recreational. More subtle and complex quality declines have also been inflicted on wetlands by both air and water pollution.

Wetlands represent very valuable natural capital assets and therefore require some conser-vation and sustainable management. A "no net-loss" policy objective has much to recommend it. This policy objective need not be interpreted in terms of absolute limits. The key issue here is the nature and extent of substitution opportunities. For some classes of wetlands, substitution opportunities may be available.

In terms of the stock of wetland assets and its sustainable management, we can approach the problem from a potential substitution perspective based on the valuation of different classes of wetland. It is possible to distinguish several management categories of such ecosystems, and this classification can be improved over time as more detailed functional assessments of different wetlands become available.

Thus, "internationally important" wetlands could be viewed as elements of the world's "critical" natural capital stock $(K_N{}^C)$. These assets are characterised by essentiality, irreversibility and uncertainty. The essentiality characteristic ensures a high total economic value, and also corresponds to a low or zero degree of substitutability. Such resources should be subject to an anticipatory and precautionary safe minimum standards (SMS) approach. Conditions of irreversibility and uncertainty reinforce an economic prescription in favour of wetland conservation rather than development. Available evidence suggests that for this "critical" wetland type, the SMS has probably already been reached.

In order to conserve such high value wetlands, international action is required, because it will in many cases be necessary to retain physically large tracts of habitats. Thus, the international support-system for migratory birds can comprise several types of ecosystems physically separated by thousands of miles. Other high value wetlands provide extended food web services, or are linked to important global climatic mechanisms (*e.g.* carbon sources and sinks). Conservation of such globally important resources must be a high priority. International conventions and global biospherical reserve designations (as advocated by the Brundtland Committee) are among the primary options which will need to be examined in this context.

However, relatively lower value wetlands could be treated as components of "Other Natural Capital Stock" (K_N), and as such may be substitutable for/by man-made capital. In these cases, some degradation or depletion may be acceptable, if the substituted assets (*e.g.* restored wetlands and/or created artificial wetlands) are augmented sufficiently. At the programme level, the sustainability constraint (*i.e.* no net-loss of the remaining wetlands stock) amounts to including within any portfolio of wetland development investments and/or investments with the potential to degrade wetlands, one or more "shadow projects" (wetland restoration and/or artificial creation). These shadow projects must fully compensate for the wetland loss wrought by the other projects in the portfolio. The shadow project options should be as cost-effective as possible, but should not be subject to the normal cost-benefit efficiency rules, because of their broader (substitution) objectives.

On the other hand, the extent to which habitat loss can be compensated for through the creation of "new" semi-natural areas closely resembling the lost asset is a complex question. Based on limited fieldwork experience to date, three reconstruction options seem to be available (Buckley, 1989):

  a) *Habitat reconstruction*; constructing ecological communities away from the site being lost due to development activity;
  b) *Habitat transplantation*; moving an original habitat from the donor site threatened by development to a receptor site;
  c) *Habitat restoration*; enhancing the ecological potential of existing (but degraded or impoverished) habitats of the same type as that threatened by development.

The habitat construction option could involve the extension of the threatened habitat (for example, the deliberate flooding of extra land close to the original wetland site, allowing flora and fauna to colonise over time (known as "habitat duplication"). On the other hand, the new (artificially-created) habitats may be located some distance from the development project site. The danger in this context is that conservation sites often need to be viewed in terms of quite extensive networks. Small, isolated parcels of conserved habitats are unlikely to remain viable in biodiversity terms.

There are at least two types of habitat reconstruction policy:

a) Creating relatively simple habitats, or habitats providing only a limited number of functional services (*e.g.* birdnesting or wintering areas); and

b) The "strong" conservation requirement of recreating the most convincing replicas of ancient and complex habitats that it is possible to achieve.

Conservationists would argue that policy mode *(b)* could best be operationalised by a strategy that re-affirmed the commitment to retain all existing semi-natural habitat. Despite the existence of some 20 conservation designations stemming from 30 Acts of Parliament in the United Kingdom, for example, important landscape and ecological sites (including wetlands) continue to be lost. The next component of the strategy would be the "duplication" of ecological communities centred around existing SSSI and NNR sites. Finally, attempts could be made to re-create appropriate habitats related to biogeographical regions (Buckley, 1989).

However, adequate substitutes may not be available, either because of physical or financial (*e.g.* excessive restoration or creation costs) constraints. In these instances, conservation of critical natural capital is a high priority, and the costs of this environmental standard/constraint can be expressed as the foregone benefits from development. The decision-maker will then have to decide whether or not the imposition of the environmental constraint is socially too costly.

In some cases, it may prove possible to augment the supply of lower-order wetlands by constructing new artificial wetlands and/or by reclaiming (or more intensively managing) existing, but degraded, areas. Current marsh establishment technology can play a positive, though limited, role. The available technology is potentially useful for restoring degraded marsh areas, or for repairing small portions of existing marshes. However, European experience, based on attempts to restore complex semi-natural wetlands in both Britain and Holland, indicates that restoration is a protracted and expensive affair. Considerable restoration success has been achieved, for example, in small areas of the Norfolk Broads by completely sealing off a Broad from the rest of the wetland system, which is heavily utilised by tourists, and which contains polluted water. Extensive use of this method in multiple-use wetlands, however, is clearly not a practical proposition.

After an evaluation of past wetland restoration projects in San Francisco Bay, Race (1985) concluded that "many of the projects never reached the level of success purported, and others have been plagued by serious problems". More intensive management of alternative, lower-order, or degraded areas of wetland, or construction of new wetlands, are not the only substitution possibilities. Increasingly stringent institutional rules covering recreational and other activities, as well as improved effluent discharge standards, could also have a role to play in some high value wetlands that are already exposed to multiple-usage pressures.

Overall, it seems reasonable to regard the majority of wetlands as natural systems, which, once destroyed, can at best be only partially and imperfectly replaced by man. Since most outright wetland development decisions are irreversible (on physical grounds or for reasons of practicability), then a strong case for wetland conservation can be made on both economic efficiency and intergenerational equity grounds.

Further, there is a need to strike a balance between wetland conservation and sustainable usage. A range of mitigative and remedial policies are required, probably tailored to suit different national circumstances. This review of currently-adopted wetland management measures indicates that some countries have enacted quite broadly-based packages of measures intended to halt, or at least slow down, wetland losses. Empirical evidence pertaining to the precise success or failure of these measures is not yet generally available.

Policy successes have probably been "patchy", depending on the country one is considering. With the exception of the wetland purchase policy, most of the other policy options do not offer any long-term conservation protection. More extensive purchasing of wetlands is likely to yield major social benefits in those countries (*e.g.* North America) with relatively extensive wetlands still intact. In regions (*e.g.* in Europe) where wetlands are much demanded, and already much transformed, the purchase option is more problematic, but it still offers some scope for increased wetland conservation. Sustainable usage and management systems are a high priority in the European countries. A promising start has been made with the introduction of the ESA schemes. But these schemes need to be refined, made more extensive, and above all else, put on a long-term basis.

Finally, sustainable usage is a key requirement for tropical wetlands in developing countries. In this context, globally significant wetland resources, will require biospheric reserve designation (or similar) status. To make such designations operational, there will be a need for international compensatory resource transfers (debt for nature swaps and/or other devices) to aid developing economies. The most appropriate type of management system for a particular wetland will depend on several factors: biological conservation needs; the wetland functions and services requiring protection and their value; adjacent land use patterns; regional economic opportunities, and (especially for developing countries) the subsistence needs of local people; and the availability of environmentally-sensitive international aid flows.

REFERENCES

Barbier, E.B. (1989). *Economic Evaluation of Tropical Wetland Resources: Application in Central America,* LEEC Working Paper, University College London, London.

Batie, S.S. & Mabbs-Zeno, C.C. (1985). "Opportunity Costs of Preserving Coastal Wetlands: A Case Study of a Recreational Housing Development", *Land Economics,* Vol. 61(1).

Batie, S.S. & Shabman, L. (1982). "Estimating The Economic Value of Wetlands: Principles, Methods and Limitations", *Coastal Zone Management Journal,* Vol. 10(3).

Batie, S.S. & Wilson, J.R. (1979). *Economic Values Attributable to Virginia's Coastal Wetlands and Inputs in Oyster Production,* Research Division Bulletin, 150, Dept. of Agricultural Economics, Virginia Polytechnic Institute and State University, Blacksburg.

Bishop, R. & Heberlein, T.A. (1980). *Simulated Markets, Hypothetical Markets and Travel Cost Analysis: Alternative Methods of Estimating Outdoor Recreation Demand,* Dept. of Agricultural Economics, Staff Paper, 187, University of Wisconsin.

Bowers, J.K. (1983). "Cost-Benefit Analysis of Wetland Drainage", *Environment and Planning,* Vol. 15(2).

Bowers, J.K. (1988). "Cost-Benefit Analysis in Theory and Practice: Agricultural Land Drainage Projects". In: Turner, R.K., *Sustainable Environmental Management: Principles and Practice,* Belhaven Press, London.

Brown, G.M. & Pollakowski, H.O. (1977). "Economic Valuation of Shoreline", *Review of Economics and Statistics,* Vol. 59, No. 4, pp. 272-278.

Buckley, G.P. (ed) (1989). *Biological Habitat Reconstruction.* Belhaven Press, London.

Costanza, R., Farber, S. & Maxwell, J. (1987). "The Valuation and Management of Wetland Ecosystems". Paper presented at the Vienna Centre Conference on Integrating Ecology and Economics. Barcelona, September.

Costanza, R. and Farber, S.C. (1989). "Valuation and Management of Wetland Ecosystems" *Ecological Economics,* Vol. 1, No. 4, pp. 335-361.

Cowan, J.H., Turner, R.E. & Cahoon, D.R. (1988). "Marsh Management Plans in Practice: Do They Work in Coastal Louisiana, USA"? *Environmental Management,* Vol. 12(1).

Crosson, P.R. (1990) "Supplying the Environmental Values of Agriculture". *Resources,* N° 98, RFF, Washington D.C.

Dossor, J. (1984). *Land Drainage Improvement Scheme for Five Mile Level: A Consulting Report,* Dossor & Partners, Norwich.

Farber, S.C. (1988). "The Value of Coastal Wetlands for Recreation: An Application of Travel Cost and Contingent Valuation Methodologies". *Journal of Environmental Management,* Vol. 26, No. 3, pp. 299-312.

Farber, S. & Costanza, R. (1989). "The Economic Value of Wetland Systems". *Journal of Environmental Economics and Management,* 24, 41-51.

41

Fisher, A.C. & Haverman, W.M. (1985). "Endangered Species: The Economics of Irreversible Damage". In: Hall, D. *et al.* (eds) *Economics of Ecosystem Management,* W. Junk Publishers, Dordrecht.

Freeman, A.M. (1984). "The Quasi-Option Value of Irreversible Development", *Journal of Environmental Economics and Management,* Vol. 11(3).

Fritz, W.R. & Helle, S.C. (1979). "Cypress Wetlands for Tertiary Treatment." In U.S.E.P.A., *Aquaculture Systems for Wastewater Treatment: Seminar Proceedings and Engineering Assessment.* U.S.E.P.A. Office of Water Programme Operations, Series Water 430/9-80-006, Washington.

Goodland, R. & Ledec, G. (1989). "Wildlands: Balancing Conversion with Conservation in World Bank Projects". *Environment,* 31.6-11 & 27-35.

Gosselink, J.G., Odum, E.P. & Pope, R.M. (1974). *The Value of the Tidal Marsh,* Centre for Wetland Resources, Louisiana State University, Baton Rouge.

Gupta, T.R. & Foster, J.H. (1975). "Economic Criteria for Freshwater Wetland Policy in Massachusetts", *American Journal of Agricultural Economics* Vol. 57(1), pp. 40-45.

Kahn, J.R. & Kemp, W.M. (1985). "Economic Losses Associated with the Degradation of an Ecosystem: The Case of Submerged Aquatic Vegetation in Chesapeake Bay", *Journal of Environmental Economics and Management,* Vol. 12(3), pp. 246-263.

Lynne, G.D., Conray, P. & Prochaska, F.J. (1981). "Economic Valuation of Marsh Areas for Marine Production Processes", *Journal of Environmental Economics and Management,* Vol. 8(2).

Mendelssohn, I.A., Turner, R.E. & McKee, K.L. (1983). "Louisiana's Eroding Coastal Zone: Management Alternatives", *Journal of the Limnological Society of South Africa,* Vol. 9(2).

Milon, J.W., Gressel, J. & Mulkey, D. (1984). "Hedonic Amenity Valuation and Functional Form Specification", *Land Economics,* Vol. 60(4).

Nelson, R.W. (1986). "Wetlands Policy Crisis: United States and United Kingdom", *Agriculture Ecosystem and Environment,* Vol. 18.

Nelson, R.W. & Logan, W.J. (1984). "Policy on Wetland Mitigation", *Environment International,* Vol. 10(1).

Park, W.M. & Batie, S.S. (1979). *Methodological Issues Associated with Estimation of the Economic Value of Coastal Wetlands in Improving Water Quality,* Sea Grant Project Paper VPl-SG-79-O9, Dept. of Agricultural Economics, Virginia Polytechnic Institute and State University, Blacksburg.

Pearce, D.W. & Turner, R.K. (1990). *Economics of Natural Resources and the Environment.* Harvester Wheatsheaf, Hemel Hempstead.

Pearce, D.W., Markandya, A. & Barbier, B. (1989). *Blueprint for a Green Economy,* Earthscan, London.

Race, M.S. (1985). "Critique of Present Wetlands Mitigation Policies in the United States Based on an Analysis of Past Restoration Projects in San Francisco Bay", *Environmental Management,* Vol. 9(1).

Seller, C., Stoll, J.R. & Chavas, J. (1985). "Validation of Empirical Measures of Welfare Change: A Comparison of Nonmarket Techniques", *Land Economics,* Vol. 61(2).

Shabman, L., Batie, S. & Mabbs-Zeno, C. (1979). "The Economics of Wetland Preservation in Virginia", *Journal of the North Eastern Agricultural Economics Council,* Vol. 8(2).

Shabman, L. & Bertelson (1979). "The Use of Development Value Estimates for Coastal Wetland Permit Decisions", *Land Economics,* Vol. 55(2).

Tchobanoglous, G. & Culp, G.L. (1986). "Wetland Systems for Wastewater Treatment: An Engineering Assessment". In: U.S.E.P.A. *Aquaculture Systems for Wastewater Treatment,* Office of Water Programme Operations, Series Water E.P.A. 430/9-80-007, Washington.

Thibodeau, F.R. & Ostro, B.D. (1981). "An Economic Analysis of Wetland Protection", *Journal of Environmental Management,* Vol. 12(1).

Turner, R.K. (ed) (1988*a*). *Sustainable Environmental Management: Principles and Practice,* Belhaven Press, London.

Turner, R.K. (1988b). "Wetland Conservation: Economics and Ethics". In: Collard, D. *et al.* (eds) *Economics, Growth and Sustainable Environments,* Macmillan, London.

Turner, R.K. & Brooke, J. (1988). "Management and Valuation of an Environmentally Sensitive Area: Norfolk Broadland Case Study", *Environmental Management,* Vol. 12(3).

Turner, R.K., Dent, D. & Hey, R.D. (1983). "Valuation of the Environmental Impact of Wetland Flood Protection and Drainage Schemes", *Environment and Planning,* Vol. 15(4).

Turner, R.K. and Jones, T. (eds). (1991). *Wetlands: Market and Intervention Failures (Four Case Studies).* Earthscan Publications: London, U.K.

US Office of Technology Assessment (1984). *Wetlands, Their Use and Regulation,* Washington.

Williams, T.C. (1980). "Wetlands Irrigation Aids Man and Nature", *Water and Wastes Engineering,* Nov., pp. 28-31.

Willis, K.G. & Benson, J.F. (1988). "Valuation of Wildlife: A Case Study of the Upper Teesdale Site of Special Scientific Interest and Comparison of Methods in Environmental Economics". In: Turner, R.K. (ed.) *Sustainable Environmental Management: Principles and Practice,* Belhaven Press, London.

Willis, K.G., Benson, J.F. & Saunders, C.M. (1988). "The Impact of Agricultural Policy on the Costs of Nature Conservation". *Land Economics,* 64, 147-157.

Chapter 2

POLICY FAILURES IN MANAGING FORESTS

by Sören Wibe*

* Dr. Wibe is Professor of Forest Economics at the Swedish University of Agricultural Sciences, Umeå Sweden. He has served as forest consultant to the Government of Sweden for several years, most recently as co-author of a report to the Ministry of Finance on Future Forest Policy Options in Sweden.

INTRODUCTION

The purpose of this report is to identify, analyse, and suggest solutions to market and intervention failures in forestry in OECD countries. In part, the report summarises the findings of four case studies carried out in the Federal Republic of Germany, Italy, Spain and Sweden. The report also makes use of information other than what is contained in these case studies.

The paper focuses only on market and intervention failures in forestry – not on all problems in forest management. One of the main premises of the report is that forestry problems, and the failures that create these problems, vary considerably among OECD countries. Forestry – and forestry failures – are quite different in Canada and the Nordic countries, compared to, for instance, those in southern Europe or Australia. A natural consequence of this is that specific policy suggestions must take account of the specific conditions of the countries in which they are implemented.

It is often pointed out that forestry is a multiple-use activity. It is not possible to single out any one objective, like sustainable development or maximum timber yield. Forests are, and have always been, of enormous importance for mankind. But the concrete use of (and utility from) forests have changed over time. These changes are reflected both in the variation of the size and quality of forests, and in their use. Long ago, when hunting was the dominant economic activity, most of the European continent was covered by forests. When farming and catteling became dominant, the size of forests naturally declined. Historically, the size of forests reached its lowest level at the beginning of the 20th century. After that, the size of the forest (at least in Europe, but probably also in the whole of OECD) has been increasing as a result of a declining agricultural sector, diminishing use of fuelwood, and increased use forest areas for recreation.

There is nothing inherently wrong in this historical variation in forest size. Within the limits set by biological necessity, it is both natural and desirable that the size of forests – and their use – will vary with demand. The use of land (for agriculture, urban centres, transport *etc.*) will inevitably continue to change in the future, so we should not think in terms of "fixing" the size of the forest at a constant level.

The most important aspect of forestry in OECD is its multiple-use character. Forests produce timber, but they also produce wildlife for hunting, or for observation, and berries and mushrooms to pick. Forests provide a home for thousands of species which would disappear from earth without the forest environment. Forests are a place for all sorts of recreation. They provide protection against flooding and the degradation of soils. There is almost no end to the goods and services produced by forests.

All of these goods and services have different characteristics with regard to their private or public nature, and whether they are priced or not. Furthermore, the demand for these goods and services varies with geographical location and time. Finally, there is often a technical conflict in the production of these goods, (*e.g.* when the production of timber conflicts with the preservation of species, or with other environmental values).

The object of forestry is – generally stated – to maximise the net utility derived from it. But, given the wide diversity of goods and services produced and the wide diversity in demands, this is clearly a highly complicated matter. Forestry activity must vary with both location and time. To achieve this variation with the minimum of cost and maximum of benefit is the core problem of OECD forestry. This multiple-use aspect is the central theme of this report.

The next section of the paper presents a broad overview of forest resource and forestry in OECD. This is followed by a discussion of some key issues in forestry, with special concentration on the question of ownership. The theory of market and intervention failure is then outlined. This analysis is then extended to include a review of specific failures in forestry. The analysis concludes with a discussion of policy implications.

OVERVIEW OF FOREST RESOURCES

This section gives a brief description of some of the OECD forest resources. A more complete description can be found in FAO (1985), and in Montgolfier and Nilsson (1990).

Forest volumes and areas

The world's forest resources consist of about 3 billion ha of closed forests. The distribution for different regions and species is shown in Table 2.1.

Coniferous forests account for only about 40 per cent of the total forest area. The vast majority of the coniferous forests are located in the Soviet Union, and in North America. The Soviet Union alone contains about one-third of the world's total forest area.

Table 2.1. **Closed Forests in the World (Million Ha.)**

Region	Coniferous	Deciduous	Total
North America	400	230	630
South America	30	590	620
Africa	2	188	190
Europe	107	74	181
Soviet Union	697	233	930
Asia	65	335	400
Oceania	11	69	80
Total World	1 312	1 719	3 031

Source: Sedjo (1987).

Table 2.2.   **Volume of Standing Wood and Production of Roundwood**

Region	Total production	Production, m³/ha
North America	577	0.92
South America	330	0.55
Africa	430	2.15
Europe	333	1.83
Soviet Union	356	0.38
Asia	902	2.25
Oceania	35	0.42
Total	2 970	0.98

Source: Sedjo (1987).

Table 2.3.   **Closed Forests (CF) in OECD Countries**

	CF in ha. per capita	CF in % of total land area
Canada	18.1	47
USA	1.1	29
Japan	0.2	68
Australia	6.8	14
New Zealand	2.2	27
Austria	0.4	39
Belgium	0.06	19
Denmark	0.1	12
Finland	4.8	76
France	0.3	27
Germany (F.R.)	0.1	30
Greece	0.3	20
Iceland	0.5	1
Ireland	0.1	5
Italy	0.1	22
Luxembourg	0.2	32
Netherlands	0.02	9
Norway	2.0	27
Portugal	0.3	33
Spain	0.4	32
Sweden	3.6	73
Switzerland	0.2	26
Turkey	0.4	26
UK	0.04	9
Yugoslavia	0.4	36
OECD Total	1.2	32

Source: OECD Environmental Data Compendium 1987.

World production of roundwood is around 3 billion m³per year, *i.e.* about 1 m³ per hectare of closed forests. Over 50 per cent of the world's total production of roundwood is used as fuel. 30 per cent is processed in sawmills, and is used either as building material, or as raw material for furniture. Only 20 per cent of total production is transformed into pulp and paper.

Overall, about 20 million hectares of closed forests are deforested in the world each year. This means that an area corresponding to 10 per cent of total forest coverage in Europe (except the Soviet Union) is deforested each year.

The size of the forests, as measured by standing volume, in OECD countries, is illustrated in Table 2.2.

As Table 2.2 indicates, the vast majority of OECD forests are located in North America. Over two-thirds of the standing volume consists of coniferous trees. The growth rate is very similar in the different regions, the only exception being Canada, which has a very low growth rate, probably due to unfavorable climate conditions, and to a traditional lack of intensive silviculture and management.

The size of the forests, measured by wooded area is illustrated in Table 2.3.

This table shows that the relative size of forests varies quite considerably among the different OECD countries. Canada has the greatest forest area *per capita*, followed by Australia and the Nordic countries. The percentage of land area covered by forests is greatest in Finland and Sweden, where forests cover more than 70 per cent of the total land area. In the OECD area as a whole, forests account for about 30 per cent of total land area. This figure alone points to the overriding environmental importance of forests.

Forest resource developments (1950-1980)

Contrary to popular opinion, the OECD forests – at least in Europe – have grown considerably during the period since World War Two. This pattern is illustrated in Figure 2.1, where the growing stock and net annual increment for the period 1950-1980 is shown for six OECD countries.

It should be noted here that the definitions of forests changed somewhat over the period 1950-1990, so that the figures for 1970-1980 are not precisely comparable to the data for the years 1950-1960. Specifically, the definition used for 1950-1960 was "Forests in use"; for 1970 it was "Exploitable forests"; and for 1980, it was "Exploitable closed forest". It is probable that these changes mean that annual increments have been applied to a reduced base, resulting in the stated increments for 1970 and 1980 being lower than would have been the case had the 1950-1960 definitions still applied. For example, data from the (uniform time series of) the Swedish forest inventory, showed that the baseline figure used for 1950, 1960, 1970 and 1980, was 90, 91, 93 and 88 per cent of total forest area respectively.

It is also possible that the FAO data do not correspond precisely with individual country (i.e. national) estimates. This is not particularly problematic in this context, because what is of primary interest here is the trend, rather than the absolute amount, of growing stock. Regardless of what particular level is used a baseline, this trend is clear: OECD countries appear to be experiencing significant increases in the volumes of growing stock over time.

The same trend is also reported in other investigations. For instance, Montgolfier and Nilsson (1990) report that the area of forests and other wooded land increased in every OECD country between 1970 and 1987, except for the USA and Finland. They also concluded that

.. 'both the volume of growing stock, and its annual increment in the forests now being exploited commercially have risen considerably in the US, OECD Europe and Japan..'.

The main conclusion is that the wood volumes contained in OECD forests have increased considerably during the last 40 years. Also (although this is not visible in Figure 2.1), the net annual increments of forest volumes have grown. Finally, the basic trend in the ratio of fellings to forest growth seems to be downward. In 1980, not one of the countries surveyed in ETTS IV (all European contries) had fellings that exceeded growth. In general, fellings were only about

Figure 2.1. **Growing stock of closed forests in six countries**

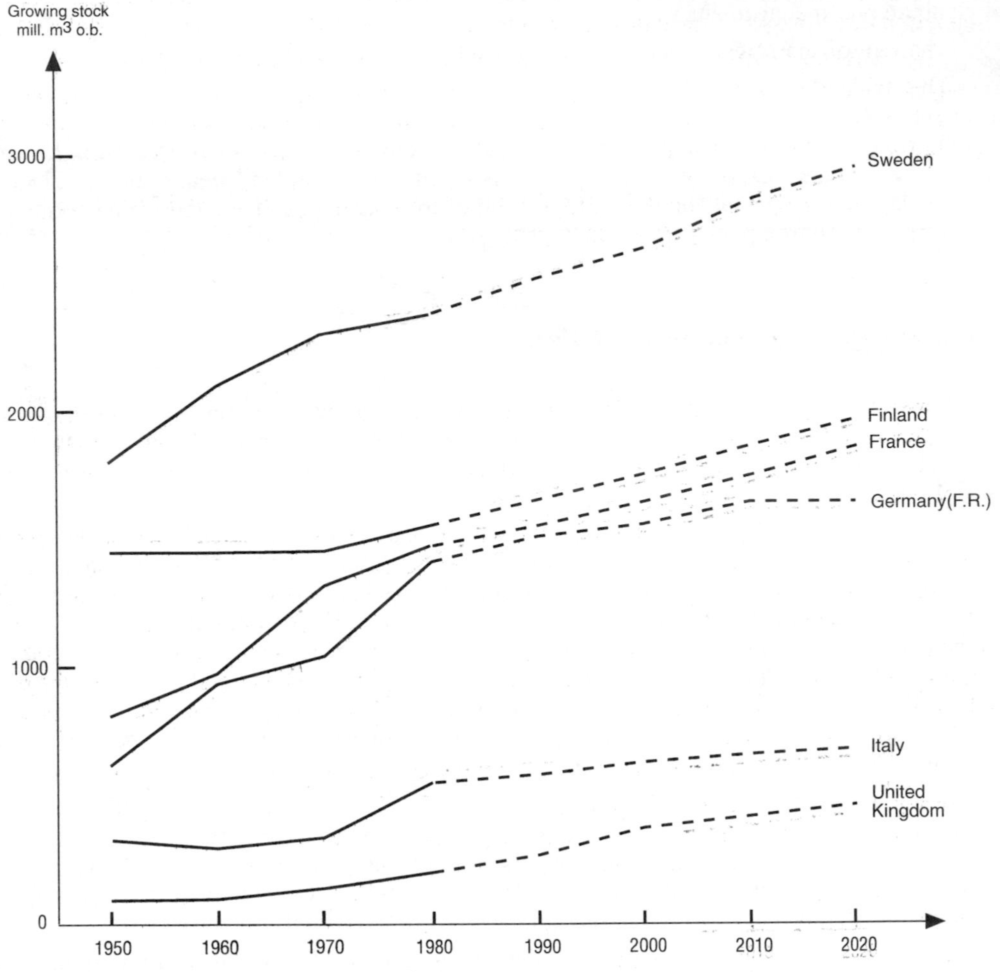

Source: FAO (1985) Annexe 5.1 Low estimate of development 1990-2020.

60-70 per cent of annual growth. Data presented by Montgolfier and Nilsson (1990) show that the annual harvest was less than annual growth for every country in OECD during the period 1980-1985. For the whole region, harvests were, on average, only about 60 per cent of growth in the period. All existing data thus indicates that total wood volumes in OECD countries are growing, and that these volumes are much larger than they were 40 years ago. Recent projections made by ETTS IV point to a continuation of this trend, with growth expected to be greater than fellings over the next three to four decades.

Age and ownership characteristics

A review of the age distribution of standing forests reveals that several countries have a significant proportion of young and middle-aged coniferous stands. The percentage of these stands reaches almost 60 per cent in France, UK, Spain, Ireland and Luxembourg. This is usually the direct result of sustained programs in these countries to increase forest plantation.

The different ownership categories and their various possessions of forest land are presented in Table 2.4.

Table 2.4.　**Forest Ownership in OECD Countries (As Percentage of Total Forest Area)**

	Public			Private		
	National	Other	Total	Farm Estates	Industry	Total
Canada	26	68	94	6	–	6
USA	26	2	28	57	15	72
Japan	31	11	42	58	–	58
Australia	74	–	74	26	–	26
New Zealand	75	–	75	19	6	25
Austria	17	13	29	71	–	71
Belgium	12	36	48	52	–	52
Denmark	25	4	29	71	–	71
Finland	24	2	26	66	9	74
France	12	17	30	70	–	70
Germany (F.R.)	31	25	56	44	–	44
Greece	65	12	77	23	–	23
Iceland	–	–	–	–	–	–
Ireland	78	–	79	21	–	21
Italy	1	39	40	59	1	60
Luxembourg	8	36	44	56	–	56
Netherlands	31	16	48	52	–	52
Norway	10	3	13	78	9	87
Portugal	3	5	9	87	4	91
Spain	6	29	35	34	31	65
Sweden	19	8	26	49	25	74
Switzerland	5	68	73	27	–	27
Turkey	100	–	100	–	–	–
UK	42	–	42	58	–	58
Yugoslavia	–	70	70	30	–	30
OECD Total	32	32	64	31	5	36

Source:　OECD Environmental Data Compendium, 1987 .

This table shows that the share of forest land owned by the public sector (state or local government) is significant in almost every OECD country. On the whole, about 65 per cent of OECD forest land is owned by the public sector, and about 35 per cent is owned by private persons and companies. The share owned by the forest industry itself is typically very low (being most significant in the USA, New Zealand, Portugal, Spain and the Nordic countries).

Economic importance of wood products

Production and employment

Forestry in itself is a fairly minor economic activity in OECD nations. For example, forestry in Italy and West Germany accounts for only about 0.1 per cent of total GNP. Even in Sweden, the figure is only about 1.0 per cent. But data indicating the direct contribution of forests to GNP underestimates their true economic importance. For example, the number of forest-holdings is large in almost every country (*e.g.* France has 3.2 million, West Germany almost 0.5 million; and Finland, Austria, Sweden and Switzerland each have more than 200 000 forest owners). The number of people occasionally engaged in some kind of forestry is large in every country.

Furthermore, wood from forestry is processed in many different sectors of the economy. Even though fuel-wood use is economically significant (especially in Europe), fuel-wood accounts for only 15 per cent of total wood consumption. Most of OECD's raw wood is used for making panels, sawn wood, or pulp and paper. This secondary processing activity accounts

Table 2.5.   **The Size of the Wood Industry in Selected OECD Countries**

Country	Number of Establishments (Number)			Average Number of Persons Engaged (Thousands)		Value Added (Percent of total industry)	
	Wood Products	Pulp and paper	Paper products	Wood Products	Pulp and paper	Paper products	Wood + pulp + paper
Austria	1 596	49	116	16	12	7	5
Canada	2 808	141	517	94	80	34	8
Finland	762	112	82	39	36	9	16
France	–	–	–	103	111	–	3
Germany (F.R.)	4 467	176	883	245	49	104	6[3]
Italy	994	178	489	43	29	35	3
Norway	841	58	64	19	10	4	4
Portugal	2 363	84	151	41	12	59	8[3]
Spain	19 330	173	966	84	18	25	4
Sweden	1 183	88	122	46	43	12	13
U.K.	6 508	291	2 007	93	34	126	4[3]
USA[1]	18 147	1 168	5 213	419	248	358	5
New Zealand[2]	1 295	19	141	16	7	5	10

1. 1982 data.
2. 1983 data.
3. Percentage of average number of persons engaged.
Source: Industrial Statistics Yearbook 1986. Vol. 1, United Nations.

for a significant proportion of total manufacturing in almost every OECD country, as Table 2.5 indicates.

Table 2.5 illustrates that the wood-processing industries account for a significant proportion of total industrial value-added (in most cases, over five per cent). The number of persons employed in these industries is also impressive. (The total number in OECD is over 2.5 million). In addition, the furniture and printing industries also use wood as the primary raw material, and the forest industry could be defined as including these sectors as well. Using this extended definition, the forest industry accounts for about 10 per cent of total OECD industrial production.

International trade

Due to the large differences which exist among countries in the relative supply of raw forest resources, international forest trade is very significant.

Table 2.6 indicates that the OECD region has an overall (forest products) trade deficit of about 10 per cent, but, by looking at the "world" balance in the same Table, it is clear that this

Table 2.6. **Trade in Forest Products: OECD Countries and World Totals (1985)**

Million US $

Country	Imports	Exports	Trade Balance
Canada	980	11 221	+10 240
USA	10 756	5 335	−5 420
Japan	5 871	770	−5 100
Australia	823	197	−626
New Zealand	113	305	+191
Austria	620	1 310	+690
Belgium-Luxembourg	1 219	606	−612
Denmark	847	181	−665
Finland	297	4 603	+4 306
France	2 838	1 577	−1 260
Germany (F.R.)	4 897	2 679	−2 217
Greece	284	31	−252
Iceland	35	−	−35
Ireland	269	33	−236
Italy	2 652	719	−1 933
Netherlands	1 872	862	−1 009
Norway	431	807	+375
Portugal	165	540	+374
Spain	711	465	−246
Sweden	556	4 930	+4 373
Switzerland	743	379	−364
Turkey	96	50	−45
U.K.	5 123	704	−4 419
Yugoslavia	278	402	−124
OECD-Total	42 490	38 717	−3 772
World-Total	55 560	49 506	−6 054

Source: FAO Yearbook of Forest Products, 1986.

balance should be zero. The fact that it is not zero probably means that different measurement standards are being used in different countries. Because the world deficit is about 10 per cent of total trade (as in OECD's), one can conclude that the OECD deficit may be ''illusory'' as well.

Table 2.6 also demonstrates that the direction of trade in forest products is, generally speaking, from the Nordic countries (Finland, Sweden and Norway) and Canada, to the rest of the OECD. However, it should be pointed out that there is an emerging surplus in countries like Portugal and New Zealand, countries which have recently been pursuing a deliberate policy of stimulating forest plantations.

Forest trade can also be divided into its major categories - paper and paper board, and sawn wood (see Tables 2.7 and 2.8). The pattern of trade changes very little, the only major exception being Japan, which has a small surplus in the trade of paper and paper board products. The general (and not unexpected pattern is that those OECD countries which are well-endowed with natural forests are net exporters of all kinds of forest products (*i.e.* from raw material to processed products), and underendowed OECD countries are net importers.

Table 2.7. **Trade in Paper and Paperboard Products: OECD Countries and World Total (1985)**

Million US $

Country	Imports	Exports	Trade Balance
Canada	424	4 793	+4 369
USA	5 426	1 559	−3 867
Japan	475	682	+206
Australia	491	33	−457
New Zealand	90	92	+2
Austria	230	647	+416
Belgium-Luxembourg	590	234	−356
Denmark	423	85	−338
Finland	80	3 060	+2 979
France	1 440	943	−496
Germany (F.R.)	2 381	1 891	−490
Greece	123	17	−105
Iceland	15	−	−15
Ireland	171	9	−162
Italy	736	544	−192
Netherlands	902	743	−158
Norway	152	533	+380
Portugal	83	91	+8
Spain	264	246	−18
Sweden	197	2 609	+2 412
Switzerland	361	253	−108
Turkey	47	20	−27
U.K.	2 668	633	−2 034
Yugoslavia	73	117	+44
OECD-Total	17 855	19 846	−1 991
World-Total	23 654	21 571	−2 083

Source: FAO Yearbook of Forest Products, 1986.

Table 2.8. **Trade in Sawnwood + Sleepers: OECD Countries and World Total (1985)**

Million US $

Country	Imports	Exports	Trade Balance
Canada	229	3 381	+3 151
USA	2 941	753	−2 187
Japan	932	15	−917
Australia	224	8	−215
New Zealand	12	61	+48
Austria	72	384	+331
Belgium-Luxembourg	239	55	−183
Denmark	222	30	−192
Finland	9	649	+639
France	340	144	−195
Germany (F.R.)	643	202	−440
Greece	67	1	−66
Iceland	11	–	−11
Ireland	56	15	−40
Italy	718	28	−689
Netherlands	425	68	−356
Norway	118	32	−85
Portugal	4	87	+83
Spain	195	17	−178
Sweden	38	1 064	+1 025
Switzerland	121	11	−109
Turkey	3	11	+8
U.K.	1 131	10	−1 121
Yugoslavia	21	164	+142
OECD-Total	8 784	7 201	−1 582
World-Total	11 277	10 117	−1 159

Source: FAO Yearbook of Forest Products, 1986.

Non-wood benefits

Non-wood benefits from forestry include both (tangible) products and (intangible) services. The products include all sorts of berries, mushrooms, nuts and fruits collected, together with the meat of hunted animals. The Swedish and Italian case studies show that the value of these products can be substantial.

The greater part of non-wood benefits is, however, realised in the form of various environmental and recreational services. Detailed descriptions of the nature of these services can be found in *e.g.* Montgolfier and Nilsson (1990) and in FAO (1985), so only a brief summary will be presented here.

First of all, forests serve an important environmental protection function. There is a close connection between forests and ''nature'', or ''wilderness''. Forests are not usually managed intensively, the way agricultural land is. Thinning, pruning and felling occur (in most cases) only once per rotation period. Forests are consequently often able to avoid man's interference for decades, and are therefore a natural home for different species of plants or animals. Thousands of different birds, mammals and insects use the forest as a home, and exist only because forests provide a suitable habitat.

Forests also provide protection from wind and rain erosion; they delay flood peaks; they inhibit snow avalanches (especially in the Alps); they help reduce noise (*e.g.* from heavy traffic); and they preserve water moisture in the soil.

The ecological importance of forests can hardly be overstated. The forest is a major determinant of the microclimate, the quality of the soil and surrounding waters, and of the biological diversity of nearby flora and fauna. The existence of vast areas with severely degraded soils (especially in the Mediterranean region) provides an illustration of what can happen when the protective functions of forests are disrupted.

It is also increasingly being recognised that forests serve an important role as gene reserves; as a source of medicinal drugs; and as natural controllers of pest and insect infestation. Moreover, the value of these particular services is steadily increasing, as countries become more and more aware of the forest's role in their provision, and as their supply becomes more and more constrained.

As an example of the environmental services performed by forests, one could consider their capacity to absorb carbon dioxide. About half of the biomass of trees consists of carbon, which was originally absorbed from the air in the form of carbon dioxide. Assuming that total growth of forests in North America and Western Europe is about 1.5 billion m^3 (stem volume, equal to about 2,25 billion m^3 of biomass), and assuming an average density of 0.4 tons/m^3, this annual growth absorbs about 450 million tons of carbon annually (or about 15 per cent of total world emission of CO_2). Even assuming annual cuttings of about 60 per cent of yearly growth, the net growth of OECD forests absorbs 5-6 per cent of the world's total annual emissions of carbon dioxide.

The recreational services of forests tend to become more valuable as larger proportions of a country's population begin to live in cities. Forest recreational services include: hiking; picnicking; cross-country or downhill skiing; horse-riding; and orienteering, among many other pursuits.

A specific kind of service is, of course, also the scenery provided by forests. In some countries this aspect has a great impact on the management of forests, and legislation on cuttings are designed to take account of these ''scenery'' values. (See, for instance, the example of the Galasso law discussed in the Italian case study.) The demand for the different types of services, of course, varies considerably among OECD countries. But the pressure on forests for recreational services is consistently greatest in the vicinity of the most heavily populated areas, no matter what country is under examination.

The relative importance of wood and non-wood benefits

The relative importance of wood and non-wood benefits varies from country to country, and between different regions in one country. It is probable that the wood to non-wood ratio is positively related to the *per capita* figure of forests (Table 2.3), and that the relative importance of wood production (as opposed to environmental and recreational services) is greatest in countries like Canada, Sweden and Finland. In countries like Italy and Spain, where people are

Table 2.9. **Use of Forest and Other Wooded Land**

	Million ectares				Percent			
	Total Area	Wood production	Protection	Recreation	Total percent	Wood production	Protection	Recreation
Nordic countries	59.8	54.1	4.5	1.2	100.0	90.5	7.5	2.0
EEC	32.8	29.2	3.5	0.1	100.0	89.0	10.7	0.3
Central Europe	3.7	2.9	0.8	–	100.0	78.4	21.6	–
Southern Europe	48.8	27.2	21.1	0.5	100.0	55.7	12.5	1.1
Eastern Europe	28.8	22.5	3.5	2.0	100.0	80.4	12.5	7.1
Total	173.1	135.9	33.4	3.8	100.0	78.5	19.3	2.2

many and forests are small, the importance of non-wood benefits is probably greater than the value of wood production.

An indication of the relative importance of the different benefits is illustrated by selected data on forest distribution according to their main function. Such figures exist for Europe and are provided in Table 2.9.

For the whole of Europe, about 80 per cent of the forest resource is used primarily for wood production; 20 per cent for protection; and 2 per cent for recreation.

It is, however, difficult to say much about the values of these services. Most non-wood services are non-marketed, and their value has to be assessed in "willingness to pay" investigations, in combination with other methods. (Indeed, some environmental services might even be impossible to evaluate.) Some "order of magnitude" estimates do exist for some of these values, as illustrated in Table 2.10, but this type of data is not generally available in OECD countries. Moreover, all estimlates of the value of non-wood benefits are crude, and many important services are often excluded from them in any event.

Of course, all figures for non-wood benefits are crude estimates and are based on subjective "willingness to pay" criteria, rather than on market decisions. Furthermore, many non-marketed services are not included in these values. But the interesting conclusion is that, even

Table 2.10. **Estimated Value of Wood and Non-wood Benefits from Sweden's Forests (Million Swedish Crowns, Adjusted to 1990 Price Levels; All Figures Refer to Benefits Minus Costs)**

Wood Production	8 000
Non-Wood Production	
Value of preserving species	450
Value of preserving virgin forests	125
Recreational value (cost side)	700
Hunting, meat value	400
Hunting, recreational value	900
Berries and mushrooms	750
Total Value of Non-Wood Production	3 325

Source: Jones and Wibe (1991).

in a country like Sweden, the value of non-wood benefits may be almost half of the value of wood production. This indicates that the non-wood benefits of forests might even be the most important factor in many countries[1]. In Sweden, at least, the value of non-wood benefits seems to be of the same "order of magnitude" as that for wood production.

KEY ISSUES IN FORESTRY

A multiple-use activity

From the preceding section, it is obvious that forestry is a multiple-use activity which produces many different products and services. There is, furthermore, great diversity with respect to the character of these goods and services. Some – like wood or berries – are private goods which can be bought and sold in normal markets. But other services, like many of the environmental benefits, are typical public goods, and have no market price.

The relative values of the different goods and services vary not only between countries, but also between regions. For example, the recreational – or scenery – value of forests might be greatest close to urban centres; the soil protection function might be most important in mountain regions; and so on.

The fundamental objective of forestry in all countries is to produce the optimal quantity of the various goods and services available from forests. This is, of course, a highly complicated matter, since it implies that forestry activities should be optimised with respect to size, location and management. In addition, optimal solutions will probably exist only regionally. For example, in some areas, a natural forest (with no management) might be optimal, while in other areas, plantation forests might be the best solution.

It is important to understand that the optimal forest management solution for a given country will not only involve an analysis of the total size of forests. It may be possible that there is a need (in terms of "optimality") to increase the proportion of land covered by forests in OECD. But the question of what *kind* of forests should exist also arises. This "quality dimension" varies not only with location, but also over time, since habits and preferences change continously. This latter aspect deserves special attention, since forestry is a long-term commitment.

Many of the problems in forestry are due to conflicts between different objectives. For instance, optimizing wood production might imply the establishment of monocultures, which in turn threatens the habitat of some species. In Sweden, for example, this conflict between species demanding natural wild forests, and a society demanding rational forestry management for wood production is seen as the central management problem facing forestry agencies. The same problem exists in most OECD countries.

Issues related to ownership

The multi-purpose character of forestry is closely connected with the questions of ownership and regulation. With private ownership, there is the problem of securing sufficient production of both public and non-marketed goods. It cannot be expected that the private owner will fully consider all public and non-priced services performed by forests. For instance, if forests close to cities are owned privately, it is not likely that they would be designed for public recreational purposes, even though this may be the optimal social use. The situation can, of course, be remedied with detailed regulations, but the private owner would then have to be compensated for the cost of adjusting to public demand. In addition, it should be noted that detailed regulations also involve their own costs.

There is another problem with private ownership that is connected to the very long production period in forestry. The optimal rotation period of forests (*i.e.* the period between planting and cutting) is determined by the Faustman-Pressler condition. In short, this condition says that forests should be cut when the (relative) growth (in monetary value) of the stand equals the market rate of interest, corrected for the fact that land not being used for a standing forest could be replanted[2].

In practice, this condition implies that the optimal rotation period in OECD forests is 60-80 years. In the Nordic countries, this figure is around 100 years. Conversely, plantations in warmer climates (*e.g.* New Zealand) often operate with optimal rotation periods of less than 40 years.

For an economic investment, 60-80 years is an extremely long period of time. The character of the forest investment is also quite special. Disregarding the costs and benefits of thinning and pruning, everything is invested at one point in time, and all the benefits are collected at some future point in time, several decades later. Normally, an economic investment yields a flow of revenue over the several years of its life, thereby reducing the total risk of the investment.

Forest investments are less attractive for private investors for two reasons. First, the exceptionally long production period involves a high degree of uncertainty. It is not possible to develop any well-founded opinion about prices, costs and taxes 75 years into the future. In addition, the biological conditions are uncertain. Insects, air pollution and other environmental problems, such as climate change, can all produce unexpected outcomes during the growth period.

Investments in forestry thus involve greater risks than those for other investments. Since risk aversion is the normal behaviour when the potential investment is significant in relation to the income of the investor, most individuals will place a risk premium on investments in forestry. The demand for a higher rate of return leads to lower investments than would be expected if the investment decision were based solely on expected value criteria. Left to the market, too little regeneration and too little reforestation will be the inevitable result.

The crucial question concerns the relationship between the size of the investment and the income of the investor. A state, or a big company with shareholders (each one which faces a negligible personal risk), can afford to disregard this risk, and look only at expected-value criteria. Large or publicly-owned companies thus have less tendency to underinvest in forestry than small farm-holdings.

The long production period also involves another problem. Even with complete certainty, it is probable that private investors would demand higher rates of return, because of the overlapping generation problem. If investors care more for the present generation (which includes themselves) than for the coming one, they will demand a higher rate of return for long-term investments. (This is because they will consider the risk of dying before the termination of the investment period.) Naturally, this risk grows with the length of the investment period, and investors will accordingly demand higher returns from forestry. In fact, even if investors cared

Table 2.11. **Main Forms of Forest Licensing in the Canadian Provinces**

Province	Management agreements				Volume licences			
	Form of Licence	Number	Term (years)[a]	Share of required harvest[b]	Form of Licence	Number	Term (years)[a]	Share of required harvest[b]
British Columbia	Tree Farm Licenses	31	25(10)	26	Forest Licenses	171	15(5)	56
Alberta	Forest Management Agreements	7	20[r]	25	Timber Licenses (Quotas)	143	20[r]	24
Saskatchewan	Forest Management License Agreements	5	20(5)[e]	93	Timber Permits	1 450	1	7
Manitoba	Forest Management Licenses	2	20[r]	60	Timber Sale Agreements	408	<15[r,h]	32
Ontario	Forest Management Agreements	28	20(5)	70	Order-in-Council Licenses	481	<20[i]	26
Quebec	CAAF Agreements[c]	300 (approx.)	25(5)	100	(None)	–	–	–
New Brunswick	Crown Timber Licenses	10	25(5)	73	Sub-Licenses	117	5(1)	27
New Scotia	License and Management Agreements	2	50(10)[f]	86	Utilisation Agreements	17	<10[r]	14
Newfoundland	Timber Licenses[d]	>100	99[g]	65	Short Term Timber	1	20[r]	10

a) Numbers in brackets indicate the number of years into the term at which "evergreen" licences may be replaced.
b) The figures shown are the approved allowable annual cut under the agreements or licences expressed as a percentage of the total allowable annual cut authorised for harvesting on provincial Crown lands. In Alberta, 43 percent of the allowable annual cut is not yet committed.
c) Contrat d'approvisionnement et d'aménagement forestier.
d) Includes a single, extensive, Timber Lease.
e) Older licences have no "evergreen" provision, but are renewable.
f) One agreement is not "evergreen", but is renewable for 40 years upon expiry of its first term. The Timber Lease has a perpetual term.
g) A few licences have 25 or 50-year terms. The Timber Lease is replaceable.
h) Term varies from one to 15 years, usually five, and is replacable.
i) Term varies from one to 20 years, depending on the size of the licencee's mill, and is renewable for one year.
r) Indicates that that the licence is renewable upon expiry of its term.
Source: The table has been compiled by Professor David Haley from Haley and Luckert (1989) and Pearse (1990).

"correctly" for the needs of future generations, the existence of an inheritance tax would produce a bias in favour of shorter investments.

The long production period is not a market failure in itself, but it produces a market failure. The outcome is the often-observed phenomenon that private forest owners tend to invest too little in regeneration and/or reforestation projects.

Uncertainty connected with forestry investments could be reduced if markets for forest land were free and perfect. In this case, an investment in forestry could be capitalised on at any moment by selling the (planted) area. But markets for land are not perfect in OECD countries. First, the buying and selling of land implies large transaction costs, especially when holdings are small (which is the general case). Second, many countries have more or less restrictive "land laws" that impose restrictions on the market for forest land. Accordingly, the imperfect market for land cannot compensate for imperfections in the investment market itself.

The problems of public ownership can be illustrated by the Canadian situation. Almost all of Canada's forests are owned by the public. (9 per cent is owned privately, 11 per cent by the federal government, and 80 per cent by the provinces.) The public sector itself, however, is only marginally engaged in active forestry, and the harvesting and processing of timber is almost exclusively a private business.

Given a situation with public ownership and private activity, the major problem is to arrange efficient contracts between private owners and industry. The existing practice is that the provincial governments sell licences on forest land to manufacturing companies for 20-50 year periods. Firms then usually obtain the right to harvest the area (once), given some restrictions on maximum annual cuts. The governments could also sell volume licenses which gives the right to cut a certain volume in an area. A summary of the main forms of forest licensing in Canada is given in Table 2.11 below.

There are many problems with this type of licensing system. First, there is the question of price. The "correct" price for the right to harvest is the stumpage value, but it is not easy to fix this price in advance. Usually, the prices are set very low, in some areas close to zero.

There is also the problem of regulating the management with respect to environmental values, future production, etc. Since the private user does not own the land, he has no direct interest in, for instance, regeneration. This has to be taken care of through regulations in the contract. However, this in turn implies a risk of inefficiency, since increased regulations usually stimulate uniformity and mediocracy in management.

There is no simple solution to the problems of ownership. Neither private nor public ownership solves all the problems involved. This is probably also an explanation for the very heterogenous pattern of ownership that exists in the OECD area.

Issues connected with other sectors of the economy

Forestry is only one part of a nation's economy, and many forest management problems are connected with conditions in adjacent sectors. The relationship with agriculture is of particular importance, since agriculture and forestry are normally the main alternatives for the use of a specific piece of land. Heavy subsidisation of agriculture means that the relative profitability of forestry declines, making forestry a less attractive activity for farmers.

The situation is almost reversed when it comes to the relationship between forestry and wetlands. Keeping a wetland open normally yields no income, and the best alternative is often to drain the area and plant forests. It is, for instance, estimated that over one million hectares of wetlands has been transformed into forests in Sweden during the last hundred years. This process continues, presently at a speed of about 30 000 hectares a year.

The most important conflict between forestry and other sectors is probably the emission of air pollutants from other sectors. The scientific evidence about declining forest health led to the establishment of the International Co-operative Programme on the Assessment and Monitoring of Air Pollution in 1985. A research programme to assess, monitor, and document the development of pollution-sourced forest damage in Europe was introduced at that time, and the first empirical investigations were carried out in 1986. The 1986 survey investigated 16 countries (this was increased to 22 countries in 1987).

The amount of forest damage was defined to be based on needle or leaf losses, or on the discolouring of foliage. The following definitions were adopted (Table 2.12).

For all species studied, the intensity of defoliation found in Europe is summarised in Table 2.13.

This data indicates that the extent of forest damage varies considerably between countries. However, the areas severely damaged (classes 3-4), are not particularly large in any country. On average, this figure is below 2 per cent, with the highest values being reported from Denmark, (5 per cent), Netherlands (4 per cent) and Switzerland (3.8 per cent).

The conclusion is thus that a very large proportion of the European forests show some signs of damage, but that the physical magnitude of severe damage is small. As a whole, the present condition of the European forests with respect to acid rain is not particularly alarming.

By comparing the two surveys for 1986-1987, it is also possible to analyse the pattern of change between the two years. Table 2.14 provides this comparison.

This table reveals that, overall, the condition of the forests in the selected countries actually appeared to *improve* between 1986 and 1987. At least, this was the case for coniferous trees, where the percentage of severely damaged trees declined in all countries studied. The decline was particularly large in countries reporting a high proportion of severly damaged trees in 1986, possibly leading to the conclusion that the 1986-87 changes are due more to classification inconsistencies than to real improvements. Nevertheless, a trend may exist. Unfortunately,

Table 2.12. **Forest Damage Classifications**

Defoliation class	Needle/leaf loss	Degree of defoliation
0	up to 10%	none
1	11 – 25%	slight
2	26 – 60%	moderate
3	> 60%	severe
4	100%	dead tree

Discoloration class	Foliage discoloured	Degree of discolouration
0	up to 10%	none
1	10 – 25%	slight
2	26 – 60%	moderate
3	> 60%	severe

Table 2.13. **Intensity of Forest Defoliation in European Countries (1987)**
(For All Species, or Only Conifers, Based on National and Regional Surveys)

Intensity of defoliation	Country	No defoliation (class 0)	Slight to severe (classes 1-4)	Moderate to severe (classes 2-4)
None	Ireland*	95.9	4.1	0.0
Low	Hungary	85.0	15.0	6.0
	Italy (Bolzano-Alto Adige)	84.7	15.3	3.3
	Bulgaria	81.7	18.3	3.6
Moderate	Sweden*	68.3	31.7	5.6
	Yugoslavia	67.8	32.2	9.5
	France	68.3	31.7	9.7
	Austria	66.5	33.5	3.5
	Luxembourg	65.4	34.6	7.9
	Finland**	65.3	34.7	12.1
	Norway*	64.1	35.9	16.7
	Spain	63.0	37.0	12.6
	German Democratic Republic	63.0	37.0	?
	Belgium	53.5	46.5	12.5
Severe	Czechoslovakia*	47.7	52.3	15.6
	Germany, Fed. Rep. of	47.7	52.3	17.3
	Liechtenstein	45.0	55.0	19.0
	Switzerland	44.0	56.0	15.0
	United Kingdom	44.0	56.0	22.0
	Netherlands	42.6	57.4	21.4
	USSR (Lithuanian SSR)*	41.5	58.5	14.8
	Denmark	39.0	61.0	23.0

*   Conifers only.
** National level, mineral soil plots only.
Source: "Forest Damage and Air Pollution", Report funded under ECE/UNEP Project FP/1 901-86-05, Geneva 1988).

improvements in the conifer situation seem to have been offset by deterioration in the broadleaves[3].

It should be added that, although some forest damages have been observed, the physical connection between defoliation and air pollution is not clear. In the particular report cited above, it is stated that ... "several countries regard air pollution as one of the main factors among the causes of forest decline, while others consider climatic or biotic factors as decisive. Interpretation and evaluation of the influence of air pollution on the health of forests differ considerably" (*op. cit.* page 47). It can be added that changes in climate (and in the age composition of the forests) are increasingly considered to be important determinants of the physical state of forests.

Canada and the USA did not participate in the monitoring programme mentioned above. However, the issue has, of course, been discussed at length in these countries as well, and several investigations have been carried out. In the USA, a cited study suggested that all forest tree species investigated (in New England), except spruce and balsam fir, were growing at rates equal to, or exceeding, those experienced prior to 1960. For spruce and balsam fir, the analysis showed that stand dynamics played a major role in the declining rates of growth. Although atmospheric deposition impacts could not be completely ruled out, the role of these pollutants

Table 2.14. **Comparison of Forest Damage Survey Results (1986-1987), Changes in Percentages of Healthy and Defoliated Trees, Coniferous and Broadleaved Species, All Ages**

	Conifers						Broadleaves					
	Defoliation classes 1-4		% change	Defoliation classes 2-4		% change	Defoliation classes 1-4		% change	Defoliation classes 2-4		% change
	1986	1987	±	1986	1987	±	1986	1987	±	1986	1987	±
Austria	36.5	32.6	−3.9	4.5	3.5	−1.0	42.9	53.5	+10.6	5.5	7.8	+2.3
Bulgaria	25.0	18.3	−6.7	4.7	3.8	−0.9	12.0	18.4	+6.4	4.0	3.1	−0.9
Czechoslovakia	49.2	52.3	+3.1	16.4	15.6	−0.8	not assessed					
France	38.0	34.8	−3.2	12.5	12.0	−0.5	19.4	21.4	+2.0	4.8	6.5	+1.7
Luxembourg	20.2	19.6	−0.6	4.2	3.8	−0.4	30.2	43.0	+12.8	5.6	10.1	+4.5
Germany (Federal Republic)	52.8	48.6	−4.2	19.5	15.9	−3.6	54.8	59.6	+4.8	16.8	19.2	+2.4
Netherlands	59.2	52.5	−6.7	28.9	18.7	−10.2	47.0	67.1	+20.1	13.2	26.5	+13.3
Spain**	38.7	31.7	−7.0	18.2	10.7	−7.5	4.2	42.0	−2.6	13.7		
Switzerland	52.0	55.0	+3.0	16.0	14.0	−2.0	45.0	57.0	+12.0	8.0	15.0	+7.0
Sweden*	47.6	31.7	−15.9	11.1	5.6	−5.5	not assessed					
Yugoslavia	38.8	45.9	7.1	23.0	16.1	−6.9	not assessed in 1986					

* 1986 figures re-calculated to conform with ECE/UN-classification.
** Due to a change in sampling intensity, 1986 figures are not comparable to 1987.
Source: ECG/UNEP (1988).

was considered to be minimal. Also, in an analysis on the causes of declining growth in Georgia, North and South Carolina, no clear and direct linkages between air pollution levels and reduced growth rates could be demonstrated. Accordingly, the results for the USA seem consistent with those for Europe. In some areas, and for some species, a declining rate of growth and an increasing number of damaged trees has been observed, but no definite connection between air pollution and declining growth has yet been established (*op. cit.* pages 41-45).

The overall conclusion is that the links between air pollution and forest decline are not clear. It is even debated if a problem exists at all. Some scientists argue that observed damages are the natural consequences of ageing forests and climatic changes (especially the cold winters in the late 1970's and early 1980's). On the other hand, some scientists argue that the present inability to link damages with air pollution cannot be taken as evidence of the unimportance of air pollution either. In essence, their argument is that there exists a critical limit. Below this limit (*i.e.* the present situation), there may be no visible signs of damage; but once the pollution limit has been passed, a dramatic decline in forest growth will follow. This position is supported by the fact that acid rain has been shown to degrade soil quality. This is particularly evident in the Nordic countries, where the soil lacks the natural "buffering" capacity of limestone. It has, for instance, been estimated that 650 000 ha of productive forest land in the western regions of Sweden are in bad condition, due to acidification.

Overall, the only sensible conclusion is that air pollution may already be (or may become) a serious problem for forestry in OECD countries[4].

The theory of market failures

   The basic principle of a market failure is quite simple, and can be illustrated with the familiar demand/supply diagram (Figure 2.2). The supply curves represents the marginal social valuation of forest production. The ideal market solution will occur at the point where these two curves intersect (*i.e.* where marginal social cost equals marginal social revenue).

   A market failure occurs where the solution actually realised in the market does not correspond to the ideal situation described above. This could happen for many different reasons, but two basic possibilities exist: *i)* the individual market supply and/or demand curves in Figure 2.2 (*i.e.* the curves that describe the relationships which actually exist in individual markets) do not correspond to the true social cost and revenue curves; *ii)* individual market supply and demand curves correctly aggregate to marginal social costs and benefits, but actual production levels are not consistent with the equilibrium point (*Q*).

   If the curves in case *(ii)* of Figure 2.2 are the "true" social cost and revenue curves, the benefits of a certain level of production can be measured by the area under the demand curve, and total costs can be measured by the area under the supply curve. It can be shown that the optimum net social revenue level will occur where the two curves intersect. (If production is lower than optimal (*e.g.* at "*X*"), a loss corresponding to the area ABC, will occur. If actual

Figure 2.2. **Illustration of market failure**

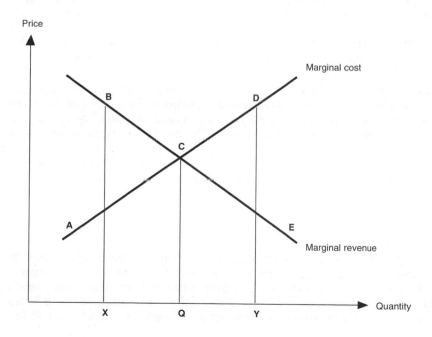

production were higher, (*e.g.* at "*Y*"), the social loss would be CDE). It is important to notice that it is only the *production* level that counts. If the price, for some reason, is too high but the production level remains at "Q", there is no social loss. The higher price implies a distributional shift between consumers and producers, but no net social loss occurs.

Some basic reasons for market failure are listed below. The term "market demand (supply) curve", is then reserved for the price-quantity combinations corresponding to actual (and observable) behaviour. "True" demand and supply curves are identical to the correct social marginal cost and revenue curves.

Non-Competitive Markets

The "classical" market failure occurs when markets are non-competitive (*i.e.* when they are dominated by one or a few buyers (or sellers), when cartels are formed, *etc.*). When markets are not competitive, firms can influence the price by altering their demand or supply behaviour. Profit maximization will then yield a solution that deviates from the socially optimal one. In the case of a monopoly (one single seller), the market solution results in a point on the true demand curve to the left of the optimum point (*i.e.* too high price, and too low production). In the monopsony case (one buyer), the market solution will also be at a point on the supply curve to the left of optimum (*i.e.* too low a price and too low a quantity).

External Effects

External effects occur when production or consumption of goods and services has (positive or negative) impacts beyond what is actually traded in the market place. The standard example is emissions from a factory that negatively influence the well-being of people in the surroundings. In the case of a *negative* external effect, the firm produces too much since the cost of the negative effect is not included in its cost function. (Alternatively, the benefits of a certain level of production are over-valued). In the case of a *positive* external effect, the "pure" market solution results in too low a production level. The logic of market failures due to external effects can also be described with the help of a transformation curve. Consider Figure 2.3.

The transformation (or production possibility) curve *TT* pictures the production of two goods in a firm (or a nation) with given resources. Good 1 is the marketed good, and Good 2 the non-marketed external effect. In this case, we can think of Good 2 as a positive effect like clean air, or "wildlife levels" of the society. The point "*A*" is the point that maximises welfare for society and gives the "socially" correct combination of Goods. But since only Good 1 has a market price, profit maximizing firms will produce the optimal quantity of Good 1 (*i.e.* at the point "*T*"), thereby causing a welfare loss equal to the difference between *UU* and *U'U'*.

Incomplete information and "sticky" prices

A third possible source of market failure occurs when producers do not know the correct shape or position of their own demand or cost curves. For example, if a producer guesses correctly on the cost side, but believes his demand function to be smaller than what it actually turns out to be, production will be lower than optimal. This situation could be varied: the producer could expect a higher demand than actually materialises, or he could err in assessing

Figure 2.3. **Illustration of market failures due to externalities**

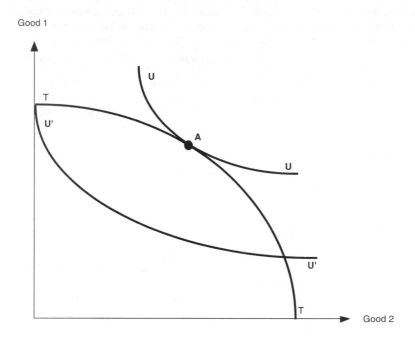

his actual cost function. Closely related to the case of incomplete information is the question of "sticky prices". In this case, assume that the producer does not know the actual demand, and that he sets his price at a certain level. He then discovers that the price was too low, but prices prove to be "sticky", so he cannot change them until next season. The production level actually experienced will then be lower than optimal.

Public goods

A pure public good is one whose consumption by one person does not encroach on some other person's consumption opportunities. Standard examples include radio or TV broadcasting; a beautiful view (*e.g.* flowers in a park); and the defense forces of a country. It is not necessary that the existence of public goods inevitably lead to market failure. But the "free-rider" problem (*i.e.* the problem of people trying to hide their preferences in order to escape the obligation to pay) makes the operation of an efficient market more difficult. Many economists believe that a complete market solution will lead to an undersupply of public goods, since the "revealed" demand for these goods will always be less than what would be socially optimal.

Intervention failure theory

Intervention failure can be analyzed in much the same manner as market failure. The point of departure is a market failure (*i.e.* a welfare loss of the kind illustrated in Figures 2.2 and 2.3). It is assumed that intervention in one form or other can correct for this loss and in the Figure 2.2 case of too low a production level, increase production from "*X*" to "*Q*". The possible gains from intervention correspond to the area *ABC*. If we assume that the degree of intervention is variable, and can somehow be measured quantitatively, (*e.g.* by the number of persons in the regulation authorities), and if we order the degree of intervention according to efficiency, we obtain a negatively-sloped curve representing the marginal benefits of intervention. To this curve, we add the marginal cost curve of intervention to obtain a demand-supply relationship for interventions. This relationship is illustrated in Figure 2.4.

Total benefits to be gained by intervention are *OAB* (which equals the size of the triangle *ABC* in Figure 2.2. It is often suggested that intervention should aim at correcting *all* market failure (*i.e.* in Figure 2.3, to increase production from "*X*" to "*Q*"). The basic error in this reasoning is clearly seen in Figure 2.4. Intervention has its costs, and the optimal degree of intervention is not at "*B*", but at "*C*" – where the marginal costs of the intervention intersect with the marginal benefits of that intervention.

In general, the total intervention policy failure is either a degree of intervention different from point "*C*" in Figure 2.4, or the inability to find a cost-efficient market solution (point "*C*" in Figure 2.2). The basic difference between market and intervention failures is that, for interventions, it is not the market, but a political process that determines the final outcome.

Figure 2.4. **Illustration of intervention failure**

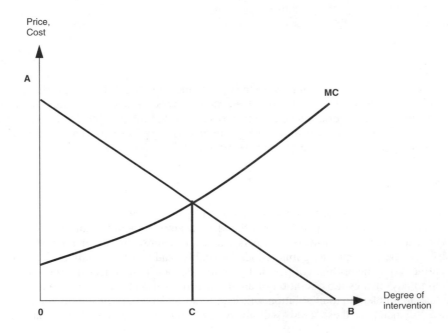

Accordingly, theories of intervention failures contain a large component of political theory, notably theories of group interests and group action. The reasons for intervention failures listed below are not complete, but they do provide a few examples of the types of failures that can be involved.

Intervention failures based on erroneous reasoning

Perhaps the most common cause of intervention failures is errors in reasoning. Since intervention is not based on a market reaction, it has to be decided within a political process, where intellectual reasoning plays the role of market prices. Many types of errors can then determine the outcome. For instance, the whole premise of an intervention can be wrong, since there is no market failure from the beginning. Nevertheless, some (influential) people may believe that there is a market failure, and want to correct it with an intervention. In this case, the marginal benefit curve for the intervention is below zero from the beginning, and there is no (net) benefit to be gained from intervening at all.

Another common error is to base intervention decisions on total, rather than on marginal cost and revenue curves. It is often argued that the level of intervention should increase as long as total benefits are growing. However, as pointed out above, the costs of intervening are also important. Relying on average or total benefits rather than marginal benefits will lead to a higher than optimal level of intervention.

Intervention failures based on group interest

Intervention is decided in a political process. Accordingly, groups try to influence decisions in their favour. If, for instance, the original market failure was due to a monopoly (*e.g.* too high prices and too low quantities), producers' organisations will try to maintain the situation, and to minimise intervention. In this effort, they will be supported by all groups which obtain part of the quasi-rents involved (*e.g.* trade unions). In other cases, (*e.g.* when an industry is protected from competition or obtains state subsidies, producers' organisations will naturally fight for the continuation of the intervention.

A not unimportant source of group interest is the regulating bodies themselves. Any bureaucracy has a natural ambition to grow, and will normally try to convince politicians that the demand for its services is higher than real social benefits might indicate. Since the regulating bodies are normally the "experts", and since the efficiency of the bureau is rarely, if ever, checked, there is an inherent bias in favour of too large bureaucracies, and (thus) too much intervention.

Intervention failures based on incomplete information

For marketed goods, the demand curve is revealed by consumer behaviour. The cost curve is revealed in the competitive process: competition drives any cost-inefficient solution out of the market, and only the efficient solutions survive. Intervention has no market behaviour corresponding to this. The demand curve has to be derived more or less theoretically. Of course, since the goods involved often are non-marketed, there is little chance that the true demand will be revealed. Political intuition and similar things have to replace consumer behaviour, and the social costs of errors can be very high.

With respect to the cost side, there is seldom competition among regulating authorities. Also, there is little incentive for the organisation to really search for cost-minimizing solutions. For instance, an organisation could have been created for the supervision of some administrative regulations. The same result might have been attainable with the help of prices, but at a fraction of the cost. However, there is little incentive for the organisation to search for such a solution. Since the real cost-minimizing solutions are not known with precision, it is easiest for the organisation to continue with existing techniques.

MARKET AND INTERVENTION FAILURES IN OECD FORESTRY

A model for analysing failures

As the four case studies have shown, there are many different kinds of market and intervention failures in OECD forest management. These include such things as: overly-rigid management laws, below-cost sales from public forest companies; threatened species, due to the destruction of natural forests; or degrading soil, due to the lack of regeneration. To simplify the analysis of these failures, a forestry management model could be constructed.

We assume first that forests produce two kind of goods (or services): "timber" and "environment". "Environment" stands for all non-timber products like recreation or the protection of soil and wildlife. We assume also that forest services are produced with only two factors of production: land (measured by hectares) and other inputs (labour, fertilizers, *etc*). Since there are two outputs, the relation cannot be of a simple production function type. But a given amount of input can be related to a specific production frontier of the two outputs in question.

It is assumed in the model that there is a conflict between the production of wood and the provisions of other services[5]. But this conflict between wood and non-wood production is not one-dimensional. It is not only a question of the quantity of wood, but also about the kind of forest, and about forest management itself. For instance, the recreational value of a forest is not a linear function of the standing volume of timber, since a forest that is too dense is an obstacle to hiking, *etc*. This complex relationship is also valid for other uses. For example, some berries (or mushrooms) need an undisturbed forest, while others might benefit from wood production as a result of large clear-cut areas.

One item of particular importance is the balance between forest plantations and natural forests. Forest plantations lead to the impoverishment of flora and fauna, and to the destruction of recreational values in a "normal" forest. These effects can occur not only in "pure" plantations, but everywhere where natural forests are replaced by deliberate cultivations. One reason for this is that forest cultivation, in most cases, means the establishment of monocultures, where one species dominates the whole stand. Another aspect is that normal forest management implies the cutting of trees at a certain age. Cultivated forests thus lack the very old (and dying) trees that are a normal component of a natural forest. Ecologists strongly suspect that the establishment of monocultures, in combination with increased shortages of "old" forests, are the main explanations for the observed decline in the number of animal species in these forests. In this case, there is a clear conflict between the maximization of wood production, and the desire to preserve nature.

Figure 2.5. **Illustration of input failures**

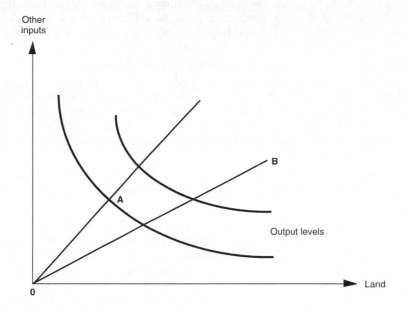

Figure 2.6. **Illustration of output failures**

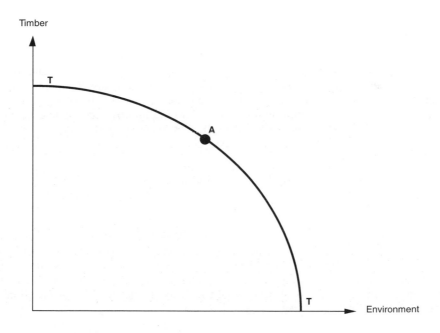

Within the model, there are four variables to be determined: land, other inputs, timber output and environmental outputs. Three types of failures can be identified. First, input quantities could be suboptimal. Second, production could be inefficient in the sense that too little "timber" or "environment" is produced from the given set of inputs. Third, output combinations could be different from the true social valuation of the two goods.

The different types of failures can be illustrated using Figure 2.5.

In Figure 2.5, it is assumed that outputs are produced in a certain proportion so that we can reduce output to a one-dimensional quantity. Various quantities of outputs can be produced by combining the two inputs (*i.e.* the "isoquant" levels in Figure 2.5). Assume now that point A represents the optimal input and production level, and that the optimal factor ratio is along the factor ray, OA. Any deviation from the input quantities represented by "A" is a failure. Two dimensions of this failure can be identified.

First, the absolute quantities being used could be wrong. For example, too little land (and other inputs) are being applied. Secondly, input combinations could be suboptimal, for instance along the ray OB:

Now consider Figure 2.6, which looks at the issue from the output side.

The curve TT is the production possibility frontier associated with a given (say the existing) level of inputs. Assume now that the point "A" is the best possible choice according to peoples' valuation of the two goods. Two kinds of inefficiencies are then possible. First, actual production could be inside the frontier, implying that more output could be "squeezed" from the same inputs. Second, output combinations as represented by the ratio between timber and environmental production might be wrong (in the sense of being sub-optimal). Below, it is argued that the most common types of failure in OECD forestry are: *i)* too little land being allocated to forestry; *ii)* too much concentration of output on timber production, compared with other (especially environmental) benefits; and *iii)* inefficient input combination processes leading to inefficient production technology.

Input failures

On the input side, the most common failure is probably that too little land is used for forestry. This is due to both intervention and market failures. In many countries in the OECD area, there is a surplus of agricultural products. From a cost-benefit point of view, it is obvious that a transformation of agricultural into forest land would improve economic efficiency. The major reason why this does not happen is state subsidies to agricultural production, in combination with high customs duties on agricultural products. This subsidisation implies a fundamental misallocation of land between forestry and agriculture.

The obvious way to correct this intervention failure would be to stop subsidizing agriculture. Another way would be to start subsidizing the afforestation of agricultural land – a solution that is now common practice in many OECD countries. However, this latter solution is inferior to simply discontinuing the subsidization of agriculture, since there are more than two ways of using land (*i.e.* forestry may or may not be the best use). Subsidizing both agriculture and forestry implies that the relative value of other land uses (*e.g.* parks) is lower. One example of this assumption in action is the subsidization of forest drainage to increase timber production. In Sweden, this type of drainage destroys over 30 000 hectares of wetlands annually. Probably only a fraction of this amount would have been transformed in the absence of a drainage subsidy.

The long-run effects of subsidizing forest plantations are also questionable. Assuming that only plantations on non-forest land (such as agricultural land) are subsidised (*i.e.* replantations are not subsidised), the subsidies would then (after a rotation period) increase supply, which would (other things being equal) lower the price of trees. Declining profitability would then discourage private investments on marginal land, and some forest owners would leave the sector after final cuttings. In the Italian situation, for example, it seems that this relationship has meant that skilled forest owners are sometimes replaced by less skilled (but subsidised) ones, with resulting declines in overall productive efficiency.

State intervention could also discourage private investments in forestry, facilitating below-cost sales by public forest companies. This phenomenon is reported from the USA, and the very low profitability of German public forests reported in the German case study indicates that this might be the case in that country as well. By permitting the marketing of timber below cost, profitability for the whole sector is reduced, and the rate of return on private investments declines.

The subsidization of adjacent sectors, such as agriculture, is an intervention failure leading to underinvestment in forestry. This tendency is reinforced by the existence of non-priced benefits produced in forestry. It is more than possible that a "correct" valuation of all these benefits (like, for instance, the carbon-absorbating capacity of forests) would lead to substantially increased investments in forestry. This latter tendency is a market failure of consideral importance. (For an example, see the Spanish case study, and the analysis of the Dehesa problem).

The tendency to underinvestment is aggravated by the "market myopia" effect discussed in the case studies on Italy, Spain and Sweden. Incomplete information about real (external) effects (*e.g.* degrading soil and sinking groundwater), in combination with increased risks associated with the long production period, is probably one of the main reasons for the vast areas of degraded soil which now exist in some areas, especially in southern Europe.

Underinvestment by private forest owners can also be explained by imperfect markets. If markets were perfect, the owner would not risk much by investing in plantation. If this plantation is correct from an economic point of view, it will raise the value of the property and the owner will be able to finance the investment (*e.g.* with a loan). Assuming perfect markets, he then has the option to sell his estate, and collect the capital gains from his plantation effort, even before the end of the rotation period. Unfortunately, markets are not perfect. Capital markets are often regulated with elements of credit rationing, and the market for forest land is heavily regulated, so that free buying and selling is not possible. These, and similar, market imperfections tend to aggravate the effects of the long production period, and to make investment in forestry less attractive for private forest owners.

It is also highly probable that forestry regulations result in overinvestments in forestry in some regions in some OECD countries. Overly-tight management regulations force owners to invest far more in forestry (or to manage the forests too intensively) than what could be justified by economic criteria alone.

There is little evidence on the under – or over – utilization of other factors. The ambitious forestry programmes of, for example, Northern Europe, and the large scale subsidization of plantations and land transformation elsewhere, indicates that the underutilization of land could partly be compensated for by excessive use of other inputs. However, as the following section illustrates, it is also probable that these interventions aggravate other problems, since they bias output combinations away from socially optimal levels.

Output Failures

In general terms, the most important output failure seems to be an overemphasis of timber production in relation to the other aspects of forestry. For instance, in Sweden, state subsidies have been given for transforming wetlands into forest land, and for forest regeneration in steep-slope regions. The latter type of subsidy has encouraged (sub-optimal) forestry activities in these areas. Since, obviously, timber values here are near (or below) zero, and because ecologists maintain that mountain areas have large environmental values, there is a strong suspicion that forest regeneration subsidies are examples of intervention failures.

It is likely that a free market solution would lead to an overemphasis on timber production. Many other benefits from forestry, notably the environmental values, lack a market price, and are therefore not included in the private profit function. This is especially true of the global benefits from forestry like the carbon-absorbation effect, the species preservation capacity, and the soil-improving service.

However, in some areas, notably in the Mediterranean regions, there seems to be another output failure resulting in too *little* timber production. As evident from the Italian and Spanish case studies, there is evidence of severe forest degradation due to excessive grazing. Grazing, uncontrolled by fences, destroys the regeneration of forests and turns the land into treeless dry areas. This process is not optimal from a socio-economic point of view, but a result of the market myopia (in combination with simple ignorance about long-run effects), and uncontrolled market forces.

Efficiency Failures

The most serious efficiency (market) failure in forestry is probably related to the effects of air pollution, which make making the soil less productive. As pointed out earlier, our knowledge of this phenomenon is very limited, and we do not know the specific magnitudes involved. For instance, we are not sure if present pollution control rates are sufficient, or if acidification of the soil will reach some critical level in the near future. Neither do we know if some part of the increased growth observed in recent years is, in fact, due to the fertilizing effect of nitrogen gases. In short, the long-run effects of air pollution on forests could be anything between "harmless" and "fatal".

There is also great concern in many OECD countries about the efficiency of smaller land owners. As shown by the Italian case study, these smallholders own a significant part of forest land in some countries. There are two aspects to this. First, small land owners might be uninterested in managing the estate simply because of the relatively small economic benefits involved. This seems to be true of many small Italian farms where the owners (in many cases, the heirs of active farmers) have moved from the estate, and where ownership is often divided among the heirs. As the numbers of active farmers decline, more and more owners are to be found among uninterested urban people. This is a long run factor that could be of critical importance in the future.

The other aspect is technical, and is due to scale advantages in harvesting and planting. If these scale advantages exist, smaller holdings mean greater costs, and an effiency loss to society. The important thing from a policy point of view is, however, not that this effect exists, but the size of it. Empirical and engineering studies of management activities (Löfgren 1990) show that the losses could be substantial if the holdings are very small, *i.e.* less than 2 hectares.

A secondary finding of this study was that cost differences between large farms and farms of "normal" size are neglible.

The existence of positive scale effects and/or uninterested small forest owners is an often-cited reason for state intervention to increase farm size, a policy now in effect in many OECD countries. But this policy might itself also lead to an intervention failure. As previously pointed out, timber is not the only important output from forest lands. There may, for example, be positive values derivable from the feeling of personal ownership associated with a piece of land. In addition, the existence of a relatively large proportion of small land-owners is a guarantee of a certain proportion of natural forest areas in the total forest "mix".

Actually, an active policy of stimulating the creation of large forest holdings might be the most serious intervention failure on the output side. Such a policy cannot be justified by normal economic welfare theory, unless there are failures elsewhere in the system which are serving to benefit smallholdings unduly.

Efficiency failures can also result from the adoption of overly-strict management regulations. One reason for this type of inefficiency is the lack of flexibility with respect to different conditions in different regions. It has been estimated, for example, that the rate of return on investments in forestry by the Swedish state forest company was 20 times higher in the south than in northern regions (Swedish Royal Academy of Forestry and Agriculture, 1988). This was largely due to the severe restrictions on, for instance, the number of plants for regeneration. It was believed by the company that it could greatly improve its economic performance without endangering either its regeneration prospects or the broader environment, if it could avoid these restrictions. The lesson here is probably that it would be better to have general (*i.e.* state) rules against the "misuse" of the forest resource, leaving all minor decisions on such things as regeneration methods, number of plants, pruning and thinning to the forest owners themselves, or to local forest management authorities.

It should, however, be clear that the total absence of management rules could also be a serious source of inefficiency. If it is correct that private investors tend to invest too little, or that they have insufficient knowledge about the biological consequences of their actions, a completely free market might lead to serious inefficiencies. Land and other resources might, in this case, be wasted, due to ignorance. Some type of management guidelines – however crude – would be preferable in this situation, to none at all.

Forestry is also sometimes used as an instrument of regional development policy. More specifically, many countries are now considering increased subsidies to forestry in remote areas as a way of promoting industrial development. However, the efficiency of such policies, as compared to more general industrial subsidies (*e.g.* a wage subsidy), can be questioned. If regional subsidies are directed specifically towards forestry activities, it implies a potential misuse of land which may not be beneficial to the overall efficiency of the forestry sector. The same output (timber, environment, employment, *etc.*) could perhaps be accomplished with fewer resources.

Finally, existing taxation rules also impose inefficiencies on the forest sector. All kinds of taxes are imposed on forestry (*e.g.* income taxes, capital taxes, wealth taxes, inheritance taxes). From published sources, it is almost impossible to compare forest taxes between countries, or to compare taxes on forestry with other activities. However, the long production period makes forestry especially sensitive to capital and inheritance taxes. It has, for example, been observed that inheritance taxes stimulate the new owner to cut earlier than is optimal, because he/she needs money to pay the tax. The importance of this particular distortion could be substantial.

Table 2.15. **Summary of Market and Intervention Failures in OECD Forestry**

MARKET FAILURES	TYPE
Incomplete information on biological consequences	OF
Uninterested and ignorant owners	EF
Scale disadvantages due to smallholdings	EF
Underinvestment in private forests	EF
Too much concentration on the production of priced products and services	OF
Destruction of ecosystems by establishing monocultures	EF
External effects from other sectors, *e.g.* air pollution	EF
INTERVENTION FAILURES	
Unequal treatment of sectors (*e.g.* stimulating agriculture, use of fuelwood, *etc.*)	IF, EF
Inappropriate use of forestry in regional policy	EF
Too tight management regulations	EF
Below-cost sales from public forest owners	EF
Heavy regulation on the market for forest land	EF
Too much stimulation of the creation of large holdings	OF

OF = Output Failure;
EF = Efficiency Failure;
IF = Input Failure.

The various market and intervention failures encountered during this study are summarised in Table 2.15.

CONCLUSIONS AND POLICY RECOMMENDATIONS

It was argued earlier that the concept of "multiple use" is crucial to an understanding of OECD forestry. Forestry is not a one-dimensional activity. On the contrary, goods and services of many kinds – private and public, priced and non-priced – are produced. The demand for forestry products is also characterised by a great diversity with respect to time and geographical location.

Because of this, it is not possible to single out one problem, or failure, that is crucial for the forestry sector. As the preceeding section shows, many different kinds of failure exist, both in the market itself and in government interventions. In this section, some policy recommendations emerging from the analysis are discussed. The focus of this discussion is on rather general recommendations, leaving specific questions aside. The discussion is also focussed on only a few important issues, rather than attempting to cover all aspects of the problem.

Improving Research and Information about the Biological Functioning and Economic Value of Forests

It is clear from the analysis above that the ecological importance of forests cannot be overstated. But our knowledge of the biological ecosystem is very limited. For instance, we do not know the long-run effects of air-borne emissions; the effects of acidification of soil; or the role of forests in the global increase of greenhouse gases. Increased scientific research would appear to be the only feasible approach to meeting this objective.

To manage forests properly requires knowledge of the biological consequences of different management programmes. For instance, it is important to know when an increase in timber production implies that certain species of flora and fauna are threatened; when a plantation programme might lead to degradation of the soil, *etc.*

Very little is also known of the economic value of all the non-priced goods and services produced in forestry. It was argued earlier that the value of the non-wood benefits might be of the same order of magnitude as the value of timber. But very few studies have been carried out in this field, and our knowledge of the valuation of the non-priced goods is extremely limited. More studies on the value of recreation forests, on the value of hunting, picking berries, *etc.,* are needed.

It is also important to improve the transmission of existing knowledge on forest biology and economies to the many forest owners in OECD countries. The number of private forest owners is large in every OECD country, and many of these owners have very little knowledge of the optimal management system. Improved information on the consequences of mismanaging the land, and free advice on matters of forest biology and economics, would probably lead to substantial improvements.

Improving the market for forest land

Many forest management problems are connected with the question of ownership. Passive ownership and small holdings are key problems in many countries. The ownership question is also connected with the over- or under-production of certain services, for instance when private owners manage their forests with the sole object of maximizing timber production, at the expense of non-priced environmental benefits.

Providing information to uninformed forest owners is one means of improving management. Another action, and one that is perhaps more important in the long run, is to improve the market for forest land. This market is now heavily restricted in many OECD countries.

There are at least two advantages to a well-functioning market for forest land. The first is that new – and hopefully interested – owners buy land from less interested ones. Interested and well informed owners can manage forests more efficiently, and obtain a greater social surplus from their forestry activities. Forest land has a greater value for interested owners, and as a consequence they are willing to pay more for the land than less interested potential buyers. A free market would lead to the selection of more interested, and more effective, forest owners.

Second, a well-functioning market could lead to changes in the geographic ownership structure that would improve efficiency. As pointed out earlier, the optimal use of forests varies with location. The recreational aspect dominates in areas close to urban centres; the species-preserving aspects dominate in ecologically-sensitive areas; while the timber-producing capacity of the forest is the most important factor in other areas. To avoid excessive regulations, it is important to adjust ownership to this structure. This means, for instance, that recreational areas should predominately be owned by the state and local communities; organizations with an interest in flora and fauna should be the owners of "natural zones", *etc.* Of course, adjusting ownership is not the only solution, but the potential gains from such policies are probably substantial.

There are many ways that this activation of the market could be achieved. One is, of course, to deregulate existing laws, but this must probably be supported by more positive actions. It is suggested in the Italian case study that the state might lease some of its forests to private non-profit organisations interested in responsible forestry for small, or even symbolic, sums. This policy could be supplemented with an active acquisition policy by the state where small and ill-managed farms were turned over (at least temporarily) to the public sector. Many other similar solutions could be invented, and adjusted to the specific situation in each country.

Deregulation

It is evident that excessive management regulation can be harmful for efficient forestry. On the other hand, given the long production period in forestry and the large number of non-priced services provided by forests, some regulation will always be desirable for ensuring the supply of ecological services (such as biological diversity, and the protection of soil wildlife and water resources).

In particular, the objective of forestry regulation should not – as is often the case at present – be directed primarily towards increasing timber production. Timber is one of few forest products that has a market (and thus a market value). Admittedly, there are several reasons why stimulating timber production may be required, but the policies that are sometimes adopted often have negative effects that outweigh the social benefits of the increased timber production.

Intervention in forestry should be primarily directed towards the protection of the many non-marketed benefits, such as the diversity of plant and animal species, recreational service, *etc.* In many cases, there is no conflict between timber production and environmental values, but in some situations (*e.g.* plantations, forests close to cities, forest wetlands) the conflict is real and sharp. In these cases, the prime goal of intervention should be to protect or enhance environmental values, since the gains from these interventions are likely to be greatest in these areas.

Many countries have regulations for stimulating timber supply. Just adding new regulations for environmental protection could bring the total amount of regulation over a critical level, to the point where the total effect on forestry could be very harmful. There are also diminishing returns to intervention, and efficiency criteria call for a careful selection of both degree and direction in these regulations.

Uniformity of taxation and subsidies

Land is a scare resource and forestry competes with other sectors for its use. To establish the best use of land, it is important that the different land-using sectors be treated equally with respect to taxation and subsidies. Presently, agriculture is heavily subsidised in most countries, a policy that diminishes the relative profitability of forestry. But forestry also has an advantageous position versus other activities in some cases, for instance when the drainage of wetlands is subsidised.

There are of course many reasons for different taxes and subsidies in different sectors. But these differences should be founded on clear and identified external effects. This is not the case today, where the positive treatment of agriculture is motivated by political and distributional factors, rather than by observed and measured external effects. Such policies eventually lead to a misuse of land. A ''correct'' policy of taxes and subsidies should aim at uniform tax and subsidy treatment among different economic sectors, – one that considers all the various potential goods and services involved.

Note that ''uniform treatment'' does not necessarily mean identical levels of tax or subsidy. As noted above, the taxes and subsidies should be (uniformly) based on real externalities, which may lead to different rates of tax or subsidy for the forest sector relative to other economic sectors. For example, the existence of many positive externalities to forestry may motivate subsidies. But these subsidies should be derived from, and directed towards, specific positive performance criteria, like the preservation of certain environmental attributes. In such cases, the size of the subsidy should be based on society's valuation of the benefit. Subsidies to the forestry sector that are not based on externality conditions should generally be avoided.

NOTES

1. See also Metz (1988), Niesslein *et al.* (1986) and Nilsson (1990).
2. This correction shortens the rotation period by 5-10 per cent, compared with the simple condition set by equalising relative growth and the interest rate.
3. The Forest Health Report 1989 for the European Community reveals no increase in defoliation between 1987 and 1988.
4. For a very alarming report see Nilsson *et al.* (1990).
5. This question was raised by Sedjo (1989), who concluded that the risk of a conflict was rather small. Sedjo's reasoning was that demands for environmental protection and/or recreation were predominantly centered in mountain regions, or other remote areas. Conversely, the forests most suitable for wood production are located on flatlands, or areas where the pressure for recreation or other purposes is not particularly severe.

REFERENCES

Bagnall, U.E., Gillmor, D.A. and Phipps, J.A. (1978). "The Recreational Use of Forest Land". *Irish Forestry*, 35[1]: pp. 19-34.

Boyd, R.G. and Hyde, W.F. (1989). *Forestry Sector Intervention*. Iowa State University Press, 295 pp.

Dowdle, B. and Hanke, S.H. (1985). "Public Timber Policy and the Wood-Products Industry". In R.T. Deacon and M.B. Johnson (Editors), *Forestlands: Public and Private*. Pacific Institute for Public Policy Research, pp. 77-102.

ECE/UNEP (1988). *Forest Damage and Air Pollution*. Report of the 1987 Forest Damage Survey in Europe, Geneva.

FAO (1985). *ETTS IV*, Rome.

FAO (1986). *Yearbook of Forest Products*, Rome.

Gregory, G.R. (1987). *Resource Economics for Foresters*. John Wiley & Sons, Inc., 477 pp.

Henly, R.K. and Ellefson, P.V. (1986). *State Forest Practice Regulation in the U.S.: Administration, Cost and Accomplishment*. Station Bulletin AD-SB-3011, Agricultural Experiment Station, University of Minnesota, 154 pp.

Johansson, P.O. (1987). *The Economic Theory and Measurement of Environmental Benefits*. Cambridge University Press, Cambridge, U.K., 223 pp.

Johansson, P.O. and Löfgren, K.G. (1985). *The Economics of Forestry and Natural Resources,* Basil Blackwell, Oxford, 292 pp.

Jones, T. and Wibe, S. (1991). *Forests: Market and Intervention Failures (Five Case Studies)*. Earthscan Publications: London, UK.

Krutilla, J.V., Fisher, A., Hyde, W.F. and Smith, V.K. (1983). "Public Versus Private Ownership: The Federal Lands Case". *Journal of Policy Analysis and Management,* 2 (4): pp. 548-558.

Löfgren, C. (1990). *Finns des stordriftsfördelar vid självverksamhet? (Scale Effects in Private Forestry).* Report No. 93, Dept. of Forest Economics, Swedish University of Agricultural Sciences, Umeå.

Mattsson, L. (1989). *Wildlife's Hunting Value.* Dept. of Forest Economics, Swedish University of Agricultural Sciences, Working Paper No. 86, Umeå.

Montgolfier, de, I. and Nilsson, S. (1990). "Forest Resource", Chapter 6 in OECD (1990). *Report on the State of the Environment* (ENV/SE/90.4). Draft version, OECD, Paris.

Nelson, R.H., and Pugliaresi, L. (1985). "Timber Harvest Policy Issues on the O & C Lands". In R.T. Deacon and M.B. Johnson (Editors), *Forestlands: Public and Private*. Pacific Institute for Public Policy Research, pp. 149-168.

Niesslein, E., Loosen, H.-J., Wilkening, W. Gunther, K. Tampe-Oloff, M. and Saile, P. (1986). *Ökonomische und politische Folgen des Waldsterbens. Europäisches Forschungszentrum fur Luftreinhaltung.* KfK-PEF 18.

Nilsson, S., Sallnäs, O. and Duinker, P. (1990). *Executive Summary: Forest Decline in Europe - Forest Potentials and Policy Implications.* International Institute for Applied Systems Analysis, Laxenberg, Austria.

OECD (1989). *Environmental Data Compendium,* OECD Paris.

Repetto, R.(1988). *The Forest for the Trees? Government Policies and The Misuse of Forest Resources.* World Resources Institute, Washington, D.C., 105 pp.

Salazar, D.J. (1985). *Political Processes and Public Regulation of Private Forest Management.* Report presented at the Annual Meeting of the Western Political Science Association, Las Vegas, 28-30 March, 1985.

Sedjo, R. (1987). ''Forest Resources in the World''. In Kallio, M., Dykstra, D.P. and Binkley, C.S. (Eds.) *The Global Forest Sector.* John Wiley & Sons, New York, 1987.

Stoklasa, J., and Duinker, P. (1988). *Social and Economic Consequences of Forest Decline in Czechoslovakia.* IIASA Working Paper WP.-88-28. International Institute for Applied Analysis, Laxenberg, Austria.

Swedish Royal Academy of Forestry and Agriculture (1988). *Regleringer i skogen - ett nodvandigt. (Regulations in Forestry - A Necessary Evil).* (In Swedish). Proceedings of a Seminar on Regulations in Swedish Forestry. Report No. 28, Stockholm.

Thoroe, C. (1985). *Forstwirtschaft und Waldschäden aus gesant wirtschaftlicher Sicht.* In die Sache mit dem Wald. BLU-Verlag. Munchen, Germany.

Tucker, R.P. (1986). *Major Sources of Deforestation in the Tropics Since 1980.* Proceedings of the 18th IUFRO World Congress, Division 6, Yugoslavia.

United Nations (1986). *Industrial Statistics Yearbook, Volume 1.*

Wibe, S. (1990). *Regulation Theory: An Introduction.* Dept. of Forest Economics, SLU, Umeå.

WHERE TO OBTAIN OECD PUBLICATIONS – OÙ OBTENIR LES PUBLICATIONS DE L'OCDE

Argentina – Argentine
CARLOS HIRSCH S.R.L.
Galería Güemes, Florida 165, 4° Piso
1333 Buenos Aires   Tel. 30.7122, 331.1787 y 331.2391
Telegram: Hirsch-Baires
Telex: 21112 UAPE-AR. Ref. s/2901
Telefax:(1)331-1787

Australia – Australie
D.A. Book (Aust.) Pty. Ltd.
648 Whitehorse Road, P.O.B 163
Mitcham, Victoria 3132   Tel. (03)873.4411
Telefax: (03)873.5679

Austria – Autriche
OECD Publications and Information Centre
Schedestrasse 7
D-W 5300 Bonn 1 (Germany)   Tel. (49.228)21.60.45
Telefax: (49.228)26.11.04
Gerold & Co.
Graben 31
Wien I   Tel. (0222)533.50.14

Belgium – Belgique
Jean De Lannoy
Avenue du Roi 202
B-1060 Bruxelles   Tel. (02)538.51.69/538.08.41
Telex: 63220   Telefax: (02) 538.08.41

Canada
Renouf Publishing Company Ltd.
1294 Algoma Road
Ottawa, ON K1B 3W8   Tel. (613)741.4333
Telex: 053-4783   Telefax: (613)741.5439
Stores:
61 Sparks Street
Ottawa, ON K1P 5R1   Tel. (613)238.8985
211 Yonge Street
Toronto, ON M5B 1M4   Tel. (416)363.3171
Federal Publications
165 University Avenue
Toronto, ON M5H 3B8   Tel. (416)581.1552
Telefax: (416)581.1743
Les Publications Fédérales
1185 rue de l'Université
Montréal, PQ H3B 3A7   Tel.(514)954-1633
Les Éditions La Liberté Inc.
3020 Chemin Sainte-Foy
Sainte-Foy, PQ G1X 3V6   Tel. (418)658.3763
Telefax: (418)658.3763

Denmark – Danemark
Munksgaard Export and Subscription Service
35, Nørre Søgade, P.O. Box 2148
DK-1016 København K   Tel. (45 33)12.85.70
Telex: 19431 MUNKS DK   Telefax: (45 33)12.93.87

Finland – Finlande
Akateeminen Kirjakauppa
Keskuskatu 1, P.O. Box 128
00100 Helsinki   Tel. (358 0)12141
Telex: 125080   Telefax: (358 0)121.4441

France
OECD/OCDE
Mail Orders/Commandes par correspondance:
2, rue André-Pascal
75775 Paris Cédex 16   Tel. (33-1)45.24.82.00
Bookshop/Librairie:
33, rue Octave-Feuillet
75016 Paris   Tel. (33-1)45.24.81.67
    (33-1)45.24.81.81
Telex: 620 160 OCDE
Telefax: (33-1)45.24.85.00 (33-1)45.24.81.76
Librairie de l'Université
12a, rue Nazareth
13100 Aix-en-Provence   Tel. 42.26.18.08
Telefax : 42.26.63.26

Germany – Allemagne
OECD Publications and Information Centre
Schedestrasse 7
D-W 5300 Bonn 1   Tel. (0228)21.60.45
Telefax: (0228)26.11.04

Greece – Grèce
Librairie Kauffmann
28 rue du Stade
105 64 Athens   Tel. 322.21.60
Telex: 218187 LIKA Gr

Hong Kong
Swindon Book Co. Ltd.
13 - 15 Lock Road
Kowloon, Hong Kong   Tel. 366.80.31
Telex: 50 441 SWIN HX   Telefax: 739.49.75

Iceland – Islande
Mál Mog Menning
Laugavegi 18, Pósthólf 392
121 Reykjavik   Tel. 15199/24240

India – Inde
Oxford Book and Stationery Co.
Scindia House
New Delhi 110001   Tel. 331.5896/5308
Telex: 31 61990 AM IN
Telefax: (11)332.5993
17 Park Street
Calcutta 700016   Tel. 240832

Indonesia – Indonésie
Pdii-Lipi
P.O. Box 269/JKSMG/88
Jakarta 12790   Tel. 583467
Telex: 62 875

Ireland – Irlande
TDC Publishers – Library Suppliers
12 North Frederick Street
Dublin 1   Tel. 744835/749677
Telex: 33530 TDCP EI   Telefax: 748416

Italy – Italie
Libreria Commissionaria Sansoni
Via Benedetto Fortini, 120/10
Casella Post. 552
50125 Firenze   Tel. (055)64.54.15
Telex: 570466   Telefax: (055)64.12.57
Via Bartolini 29
20155 Milano   Tel. 36.50.83
La diffusione delle pubblicazioni OCSE viene assicurata
dalle principali librerie ed anche da:
Editrice e Libreria Herder
Piazza Montecitorio 120
00186 Roma   Tel. 679.46.28
Telex: NATEL I 621427
Libreria Hoepli
Via Hoepli 5
20121 Milano   Tel. 86.54.46
Telex: 31.33.95   Telefax: (02)805.28.86
Libreria Scientifica
Dott. Lucio de Biasio 'Aeiou'
Via Meravigli 16
20123 Milano   Tel. 805.68.98
Telefax: 800175

Japan – Japon
OECD Publications and Information Centre
Landic Akasaka Building
2-3-4 Akasaka, Minato-ku
Tokyo 107   Tel. (81.3)3586.2016
Telefax: (81.3)3584.7929

Korea – Corée
Kyobo Book Centre Co. Ltd.
P.O. Box 1658, Kwang Hwa Moon
Seoul   Tel. (REP)730.78.91
Telex: 735.0030

Malaysia/Singapore – Malaisie/Singapour
Co-operative Bookshop Ltd.
University of Malaya
P.O. Box 1127, Jalan Pantai Baru
59700 Kuala Lumpur
Malaysia   Tel. 756.5000/756.5425
Telefax: 757.3661
Information Publications Pte. Ltd.
Pei-Fu Industrial Building
24 New Industrial Road No. 02-06
Singapore 1953   Tel. 283.1786/283.1798
Telefax: 284.8875

Netherlands – Pays-Bas
SDU Uitgeverij
Christoffel Plantijnstraat 2
Postbus 20014
2500 EA's-Gravenhage   Tel. (070 3)78.99.11
Voor bestellingen: Tel. (070 3)78.98.80
Telex: 32486 stdru   Telefax: (070 3)47.63.51

New Zealand – Nouvelle-Zélande
GP Publications Ltd.
Customer Services
33 The Esplanade - P.O. Box 38-900
Petone, Wellington
Tel. (04)685-555   Telefax: (04)685-333

Norway – Norvège
Narvesen Info Center - NIC
Bertrand Narvesens vei 2
P.O. Box 6125 Etterstad
0602 Oslo 6   Tel. (02)57.33.00
Telex: 79668 NIC N   Telefax: (02)68.19.01

Pakistan
Mirza Book Agency
65 Shahrah Quaid-E-Azam
Lahore 3   Tel. 66839
Telex: 44886 UBL PK. Attn: MIRZA BK

Portugal
Livraria Portugal
Rua do Carmo 70-74, Apart. 2681
1117 Lisboa Codex   Tel.: 347.49.82/3/4/5
Telefax: (01) 347.02.64

Singapore/Malaysia – Singapour/Malaisie
See "Malaysia/Singapore" – Voir «Malaisie/Singapour»

Spain – Espagne
Mundi-Prensa Libros S.A.
Castelló 37, Apartado 1223
Madrid 28001   Tel. (91) 431.33.99
Telex: 49370 MPLI   Telefax: 575.39.98
Libreria Internacional AEDOS
Consejo de Ciento 391
08009 - Barcelona   Tel. (93) 301-86-15
    Telefax: (93) 317-01-41
Llibreria de la Generalitat
Palau Moja, Rambla dels Estudis, 118
08002 - Barcelona   Telefax: (93) 412.18.54
Tel. (93) 318.80.12 (Subscripcions)
(93) 302.67.23 (Publicacions)

Sri Lanka
Centre for Policy Research
c/o Mercantile Credit Ltd.
55, Janadhipathi Mawatha
Colombo 1   Tel. 438471-9, 440346
Telex: 21138 VAVALEX CE   Telefax: 94.1.448900

Sweden – Suède
Fritzes Fackboksföretaget
Box 16356, Regeringsgatan 12
103 27 Stockholm   Tel. (08)23.89.00
Telex: 12387   Telefax: (08)20.50.21
Subscription Agency/Abonnements:
Wennergren-Williams AB
Nordenflychtsvägen 74, Box 30004
104 25 Stockholm   Tel. (08)13.67.00
Telex: 19937   Telefax: (08)618.62.32

Switzerland – Suisse
OECD Publications and Information Centre
Schedestrasse 7
D-W 5300 Bonn 1 (Germany)   Tel. (49.228)21.60.45
Telefax: (49.228)26.11.04
Librairie Payot
6 rue Grenus
1211 Genève 11   Tel. (022)731.89.50
Telex: 28356
Subscription Agency – Service des Abonnements
Naville S.A.
7, rue Lévrier
1201 Genève   Tél.: (022) 732.24.00
Telefax: (022) 738.48.03
Maditec S.A.
Chemin des Palettes 4
1020 Renens/Lausanne   Tel. (021)635.08.65
Telefax: (021)635.07.80
United Nations Bookshop/Librairie des Nations-Unies
Palais des Nations
1211 Genève 10   Tel. (022)734.14.73
Telex: 412962   Telefax: (022)740.09.31

Taiwan – Formose
Good Faith Worldwide Int'l. Co. Ltd.
9th Floor, No. 118, Sec. 2
Chung Hsiao E. Road
Taipei   Tel. 391.7396/391.7397
Telefax: (02) 394.9176

Thailand – Thaïlande
Suksit Siam Co. Ltd.
1715 Rama IV Road, Samyan
Bangkok 5   Tel. 251.1630

Turkey – Turquie
Kültur Yayinlari Is-Türk Ltd. Sti.
Atatürk Bulvari No. 191/Kat. 21
Kavaklidere/Ankara   Tel. 25.07.60
Dolmabahce Cad. No. 29
Besiktas/Istanbul   Tel. 160.71.88
Telex: 43482B

United Kingdom – Royaume-Uni
HMSO
Gen. enquiries   Tel. (071) 873 0011
Postal orders only:
P.O. Box 276, London SW8 5DT
Personal Callers HMSO Bookshop
49 High Holborn, London WC1V 6HB
Telex: 297138   Telefax: 071 873 2000
Branches at: Belfast, Birmingham, Bristol, Edinburgh,
Manchester

United States – États-Unis
OECD Publications and Information Centre
2001 L Street N.W., Suite 700
Washington, D.C. 20036-4910   Tel. (202)785.6323
Telefax: (202)785.0350

Venezuela
Libreria del Este
Avda F. Miranda 52, Aptdo. 60337, Edificio Galipán
Caracas 106   Tel. 951.1705/951.2307/951.1297
Telegram: Libreste Caracas

Yugoslavia – Yougoslavie
Jugoslovenska Knjiga
Knez Mihajlova 2, P.O. Box 36
Beograd   Tel.: (011)621.992
Telex: 12466 jk bgd   Telefax: (011)625.970

Orders and inquiries from countries where Distributors
have not yet been appointed should be sent to: OECD
Publications Service, 2 rue André-Pascal, 75775 Paris
Cedex 16, France.

Les commandes provenant de pays où l'OCDE n'a pas
encore désigné de distributeur devraient être adressées à :
OCDE, Service des Publications, 2, rue André-Pascal,
75775 Paris Cédex 16, France.

75880-7/91

OECD PUBLICATIONS, 2 rue André-Pascal, 75775 PARIS CEDEX 16
PRINTED IN FRANCE
(97 92 02 1) ISBN 92-64-13610-X - No. 45771 1992